# HAPPINESS GATE
#1

# HAPPINESS GATE
# #1

Khaled Al Judaia

Translated from Arabic by
Patricia Moukarzel

HAPPINESS GATE #1
Khaled Al Judaia

Published by Nomad Publishing in 2023
Email: info@nomad-publishing.com
www.nomad-publishing.com

Cover design: Lucie Wimetz

ISBN 9781914325441

© Khaled Al Judaia 2023

 The Publishers would like
to thank the Harf Literary Agency

Disclaimer: The content and any opinions included in such content reflect the views and opinions of the author and do not reflect the opinions and beliefs of the publisher, the translator, Tarjim program, or any of their affiliates. The author is solely responsible for any statements made in such content and any translation is made based on the perception of the author from the original language or source of information prior to any translation or adaptation made.

# Contents

| | |
|---|---|
| Introduction | 11 |
| What Is the Number One Gate to Happiness? | 13 |

## HUMAN FEELINGS — 15

| | |
|---|---|
| You Are Only Human | 17 |
| When We Were Young | 19 |
| Don't Fill Your Heart with Sadness | 21 |
| Release Your Anger in a Positive Way | 23 |
| Accepting Feelings Doesn't Mean Surrendering to Them, but Acting Positive | 25 |

## HAPPINESS — 28

| | |
|---|---|
| Happiness Starts with Us | 29 |
| What Is Happiness? | 31 |
| You Can't Stop the Waves, but You Can Learn to Swim | 33 |
| Unhappy Thoughts, Happy Thoughts | 35 |
| What Makes You Happy Might Make Me Sad! | 36 |
| Why Do I Want to Be Happy? | 38 |

## YOUR HAPPINESS IS UNDER YOUR CONTROL     42

    Your Thoughts Determine
    Your Quality of Life     43
    You Control 40%     45
    From 40% to 100%!     49

## YOUR CIRCUMSTANCES, A CROSSROADS, AND YOUR CHOICE     52

    Problems and Misfortunes Can Be Motivating     53
    Psychological Flexibility Lays
    the Foundation for Your Strength
    and Personality     55
    The Way We Handle a Problem Impacts Our
    Health and Our Life     57
    The Most Flexible Trees     60
    Your Treasure Is Hidden
    Under Your Rock     63
    Flexibility Improves Your Strength and Your Personality     65

## YOU ATTRACT WHAT YOU FOCUS ON     73

    You Always Get More
    of What You Focus on     74
    Your focus Makes Your Happiness
    and Your Life     76
    Reverse the Telescope     78
    What You See Is What You Get     80
    Happy Thoughts     83

## PRESERVE YOUR STRENGTH — 85

- I Won't Give Up My Strength — 86
- Live According to the Principle that "No One Is Coming" — 88
- The Results You Get = Circumstances + Your Response — 90
- Our Areas of Responsibility — 94
- It's My Father's Fault — 98
- Happy Thoughts — 100

## POSITIVE FEELINGS ARE THE PATH TO HAPPINESS — 102

- What Are You Nourishing? — 103
- Positive Feelings — 105
- Positive Feelings Broaden Your Horizons — 109
- Eliminate 100% of Your Negative Feelings — 113
- Your Positivity Ratio — 116

## LIVE YOUR FEELINGS, BE HAPPY — 121

- Appreciate the Little Pleasures — 122
- Don't Wait for a Miracle to Be Happy — 124
- Create Your Own Happy Occasions — 126

## LIVE YOUR FEELINGS, BE THANKFUL — 129

- Count Your Blessings — 130
- Gratitude Is the Way to Happiness — 132
- Appreciate Your Blessings — 134
- Bad Habits — 137

## LIVE YOUR FEELINGS: WONDER, INSPIRATION    142
- Be Amazed, Don't Be Rigid    143
- Anything Can Inspire You    150
- Fivefold Inspiration    153

## LIVE YOUR FEELINGS, BE OPTIMISTIC    158
- Optimism    159
- Optimists    161
- Why Be Optimistic?    163
- The Optimism Blend    166
- Obstacles to Optimism    172
- Happy Thoughts    178

## LIVE YOUR FEELINGS / PASSION    181
- Your Passion    182
- Passion Drives You Even in Moments of Weakness    184
- From the Chicken Coop    188

## YOUR PERSONAL STRENGTH    191
- Don't Strain Your Eyes    192
- The Negativity Bias    194
- Thinking Traps: Generalization, Omission, Distortion    196
- The Positivity Seeker and the Negativity Seeker    201
- Lean Towards Positivity    206
- Minds Are Like Computers    212
- The Present Moment Is the Key to Happiness    215

| | |
|---|---|
| The Inner Mirror | 219 |
| The Self-Esteem Quartet | 222 |
| Cut the Imaginary Ropes | 226 |

## WITH OTHERS    230
| | |
|---|---|
| The Boy Who Profited from His Father's Actions | 231 |
| You're Helping Yourself | 233 |
| From $27 to $100,000 | 237 |
| The Last Ride of the Night | 240 |
| Giving and Taking | 243 |
| Half a Medal Is Better Than no Medal | 246 |
| The Quintet of Great Relationships | 248 |

## YOUR GOALS ARE YOUR FUTURE: NO GOALS, NO HAPPINESS    252
| | |
|---|---|
| Break the Branch | 253 |
| Life Begins Outside the Comfort Zone | 255 |
| Circles of Life | 257 |
| Goals bring Happiness | 264 |
| The Law of Exponential Growth | 268 |
| Growth Mindset and Fixed Mindset | 271 |
| Don't Give Up | 275 |

# Introduction

Everyone is on a quest for happiness: the rich and the poor, the weak and the strong, the old and the young. Everything we do in life, we do for one reason only, and that is to achieve happiness. The rich don't seek money for the sake of money, but rather to be happy. And the world follows them eagerly in their endeavour, because they're fuelled by passion, and that is one way of feeling happiness. A mother and a father exert themselves and endure hardships to see their child succeed in this world; this love and sacrifice are two pillars of happiness. The same goes for a patient fighting sickness: he only does so because he has a seed of happiness in him, the seed of hope.

Not only does happiness grant us a better life and help us succeed in our relationships as well as our jobs, it also gives us enough flexibility to handle life's difficulties and crises. The search for happiness is a human desire, a religious duty even! Indeed, some of us might mistake the search for happiness for luxury, or plain selfishness. They would be wrong, because an unhappy person is shut off from the world and on bad terms with those closest to him, as well as others! Some of us may run away from the reality of our search for happiness. For example, when asked if they wanted to be happy, some people answered, "No." However, when asked if they wanted their children to be happy, their answer was a resounding, "Yes, of course."

The research on the subject of happiness, the attempts to figure out its root causes and the way to attain it are still a topic of interest for many writers, speakers and scientists. But what happened over the past ten years caused a revolution in the world of happiness; why? You will find the answer in this book, which gathers the most recent scientific findings on the subject of happiness, as well as many inspirational and touching stories that will help you learn how to sow the seeds of happiness in your life.

While reading this book, you will notice a structure that helps you "develop your happiness", by presenting each idea on happiness through a combination of four segments:

- ➤ **A story:** new chapters often start with one, whose main idea revolves around one of the topics of happiness.
- ➤ **The idea of happiness:** at the end of the story, the idea of happiness is addressed in a manner that instils it deep within you.
- ➤ **What should I do:** this segment is often included as training to transform the idea of happiness into a habit.
- ➤ **What should I read:** here, a book or scientific research is suggested on the subject of happiness for further reading.

# What is the Number One Gate to Happiness?

The main gate to happiness, around which this book revolves, is none other than you! The first gate to happiness for any human being is himself. Happiness begins when he starts understanding himself, changing and developing himself, and knowing what makes him happy. There is no one else on earth who can make you happy or sad, but you. You are the main reason, the captain of your own happiness ship. No person, place, or thing, can have power over you if you don't hand it over. That is why the main focus of this book is you, dear reader; how you can change in order to change your life for the better. You can try changing people around you, whether at home, at work, or with friends. The result won't be satisfying because changing people isn't in your hands nor mine, but in the hands of those people themselves, God willing. You can also wait for other people to make you happy, but you would be waiting a long time. Indeed, none other than you can take you to the island of happiness; happiness is your responsibility. If you make yourself happy and understand yourself, your happiness will radiate all around you, bathing your relationships, your goals, your friends, your family and everything else in your light. Thus, you will become someone who not only benefits himself but whose benefits extend to those around him.

Ultimately, gratitude is one of the feelings that make humans the happiest. So, after thanking God, I would like to thank my dear parents for lighting up my life with happiness; for teaching me how to be patient, thankful and giving. I would also like to thank my dear wife for tirelessly accompanying me on my life journey, and my son Dakhil, who brightened my existence with his kindness and his righteousness. Thank you as well to Khaled al-Otaibi, who was with me every step I made, and whose efforts played a big part in this book's success.

# HUMAN FEELINGS

1. You Are Only Human
2. When We Were Young
3. Don't Fill Your Heart with Sadness
4. Release Your Anger in a Positive Way
5. Accepting Feelings Doesn't Mean Surrendering to Them, but Acting Positively

# You Are Only Human

Strength isn't to refrain from crying. Real strength is the ability to cry, and laugh, and be afraid, or sad, or brave, at the right time. Release your feelings and you will be relieved.

**That's what happened**
A man told his story with a friend of his. He said: "My friend was being extremely selfish. My subconscious was storing a huge amount of resentment and anger towards that friend and I was repressing my feelings about him. These feelings ended up blowing up in my son's face, when he started acting like my friend.

Thank God, I quickly became aware of the problem, which first helped me calm my anger. Then, I was able to choose what to say and do to repair my relationship with my son, and to talk to him in a calm and effective way that would make him realise his selfishness, and reject it.

This extreme anger came as a result of repressing my feelings around my friend, instead of acknowledging them and releasing them in a constructive way. Had I been honest with my friend, my inner anger wouldn't have piled up and come out in front of my defenceless son!

This experience has undoubtedly changed my life; a change that will lessen the chances of me having another fit of anger in a similar situation.

When you repress your feelings, you might become

a ticking timebomb that can go off at any moment and explode in front of the wrong person. And so, I have learned that strength isn't repressing your feelings. Strength is the ability to cry, and laugh, and be afraid, or sad, or brave, at the right time and in the right way."

# When We Were Young

When we were children, we had innate feelings and we acknowledged them. We accepted our feelings: we would laugh, and be happy, and cry, and get angry, and hate, without rejecting these feelings. And we wouldn't let them linger for too long, which is why our feelings became more flexible, and neither sadness, nor crying, fear or hate got blown out of proportion. It's common to see two children fight then, a few minutes later, play together happily. We lost this flexibility, however, when we grew up and tried to suppress these feelings, to deny them and run from them. As a result, they started piling up inside us and we started to fear a lot, to hate for a long time, to worry for no reason and to grieve forever!

***Accept your feelings fully; because when you do, they will gradually decrease, and more importantly, they will have less control over you.***

Thus, accept your feelings fully; because when you do, they will gradually decrease, and more importantly, they will have less control over you. Look at the Master of all men, the most merciful, the people's teacher and the best of them in character, as well as the happiest. He still feels anger, sadness and pain, but they are positive feelings fuelled by faith.

- The Prophet (peace be upon him) was sad when his son died. Abd al-Rahman Ibn Awf saw him tear up, and he exclaimed, "O Messenger of Allah, you too weep!" So he answered, "O Ibn Awf! It is mercy." Then, he added, "The eyes are shedding tears and the heart is grieved, and we will not say except what pleases our God. O Ibrahim! Indeed we are grieved by your departure." He allowed his human feelings to come out; he wasn't callous, nor did he play pretend. But this sadness did not deviate him from the right path, with righteous manners and a positive soul that accepts God's will.
- The Prophet got very angry when a man came to him and told him that he was late for prayer because Mu'adh was taking too long, but this anger is a positive one. It's anger out of the fear of alienating people; it's an anger that educates, that is devoid of hate and exaggeration. He said three times, "O Mu'adh, do you want to cause hardship to the people?" Then he continued, "Why don't you recite 'Glorify the Name of your God, the Most High' and 'By the sun and its brightness'."
- The Prophet feared for his life, and opened up to Khadija about it, saying, "I fear that something may happen to me." Khadija replied, "Never! By Allah, Allah will never disgrace you. You keep good relations with your kith and kin, help the poor and the destitute, serve your guests generously and assist the deserving calamity-afflicted ones."

# Don't Fill Your Heart with Sadness

When your heart is filled with sadness, grief, anger, despair and you continue to bury these feelings, locking them away in your heart instead of expressing them, then you are running away from your life; from your reality. Even worse, you are strengthening their hold over you. Instead, listen to your sadness. Give yourself the chance to express whatever anger, pain and fear are buried inside you. In doing so, you will find strength. You will find the strength when you invite a friend over and share your feelings with him, or when your write them down and let them go. Know that you are moving forward with your life, that there is a bright side casting its light on you; so make the decision to walk on that bright side. No matter how many hardships you face, in the end there will be success, relief and a smile. Don't run away from your feelings, don't suppress them, and don't blame others.

***Everything that happens to you is God-given and in your best interest, if you understand the reasons behind it.***

Remember that everything that happens to you is God-given and in your best interest, if you understand the reasons behind it. Also remember that every new day is an opportunity to appreciate yourself, to stay alert, ready to face anything that comes your way.

### *Rage turned inward is called ulcers and cancer and things like that.*

Don't suppress your feelings: concealing them might lead to a setback or put pressure on your inner self. When you express your sadness-filled self, however, you take a load off it, which ultimately gives you some comfort. Release your anger in a constructive way, because "rage turned inward is called ulcers and cancer and things like that," as Marianne Williamson says. In fact, many studies have proven that writing down your negative feelings contributes to diminishing them and limiting their effects. Similarly, writing down your positive feelings reinforces them and embeds them in you and in your life. As a matter of fact, scientists performed brain scans to measure the neural activity of a group who wrote down their feelings for twenty minutes a day for an entire week. They discovered that their feelings became stronger and they themselves became calmer, with a higher tolerance.

# Release Your Anger in a Positive Way

One way to successfully get rid of negative feelings is talking to your friends about them. Don't bottle your feelings up, because it's not the appropriate behaviour and might lead to problems in the long run. Look for someone you feel close to, and with whom you're comfortable talking, and tell him everything going on in your head with complete honesty. Express your feelings; afterwards, you will feel a huge relief. But be careful: not every feeling can be discussed.

Speak openly and freely with the person who upset you, explaining your anger:

Your behaviour angered me, because…

What you did upset me, because…

Once you have expressed your anger, let it go, forgive and go your own way. Thus, you will feel relieved and free, since you did what you could; and God will reward your good intentions.

***Happiness isn't the complete absence of negative feelings, happiness is turning such feelings into a positive experience.***

The most important aspect of expressing your feelings is to not harbour any ill intentions, nor pose a threat to others.

Remember, happiness isn't the complete absence of

negative feelings, since anger is inescapable; for example, when it's a natural reaction. Happiness… happiness is turning such feelings into a positive experience.

Accept your feelings… Release them and fill your life with love, forgiveness and contentment; for suppressed feelings lead to despair. Forgive yourself, as well as others, and your life will change for the better.

# Accepting Feelings Doesn't Mean Surrendering to Them, but Acting Positive

One thing that destroys us as well as our relationships is letting our feelings control our life and our behaviour. Unfortunately, this is the case for a lot of people nowadays.

If they feel angry, they act out in anger.

If they are upset with someone, they hurt, abandon or resent them.

If they face any trivial situation, they spend the rest of their day troubled and anxious.

*There is a difference between accepting feelings, and surrendering to them.*

There is a difference between accepting feelings and surrendering to them. When his son passed away, the Prophet (peace be upon him) was bereaved and he embraced those feelings of grief. In fact, he acknowledged them by saying, "We are grieved." However, he didn't give in to sadness, stating, "But we say only what our God is pleased with." This is the positive attitude in the face of negative feelings. Likewise, accepting anger does not mean surrendering to it. Indeed, there is a difference between accepting feelings of anger that arose from a situation you experienced – which is normal – and giving in to anger by lashing out – which is bad.

Accepting anger means realising you're angry and admitting these feelings, which is a type of emotional intelligence. Whereas acting out in anger means your feelings got the best of you and you let them.

People are usually between two extremes and a middle.

There are those who suppress their feelings, letting them consume them from within.

And there are those who behave badly.

The right way of dealing with feelings is to act positive. Say you're angry at someone, so you either hide your feelings and learn to be helpless when facing them. Or you let them out in a negative way and they affect your life in a bad way.

***When you learn to admit and release your feelings… you will have an easier time controlling your anger, instead of having it control you.***

Admit your feelings and don't act out in anger. Look for the right way to act positive.

Don't react right away.

Seek refuge from the devil.

Speak openly and freely with the person who upset you.

Forgive, let go and go your own way.

Exercise.

Put off your answer for 24 hours.

That way, you go from being weak in the face of your feelings to being strong and in control; this is emotional intelligence.

I remember someone telling me this story. He said: "I received a hurtful message from one of my friends, containing bad words and accusations." He continued: "I wrote an even worse reply, but before pressing the 'Send' button, I stopped and decided to wait 24 hours.

Twenty-four hours later, I read the message I was going to send, and was struck by the angry, accusatory words in it. I rewrote my message, modifying half its content and deleting the other half, then sent it. I got a shy reply and an apology from the other person."

## What should I do?

This week, whenever something happens that worries, scares or saddens you, accept your feelings. Don't reject these feelings or ignore them. Discuss them.

Share them with a friend.

Be sad.

Write them on a piece of paper, then tear it up.

Pray to God.

Put off your answer.

Act positive.

When you accept your feelings and deal with them, their load will lessen.

## Scientific study:

A study by Dr Wegner in 1994 confirmed that when we try to suppress some of our feelings, their influence only grows stronger.

Study name: "Ironic Processing".

## What should I read?

*Feel the Fear and Do It Anyway* by Susan Jeffers.

# HAPPINESS

6. Happiness Starts with Us
7. What Is Happiness?
8. You Can't Stop the Waves, but You Can Learn to Swim…
9. Unhappy Thoughts, Happy Thoughts…
10. What Makes You Happy Might Make Me Sad…
11. Why Do I Want to Be Happy?

containing bad words and accusations." He continued: "I wrote an even worse reply, but before pressing the 'Send' button, I stopped and decided to wait 24 hours.

Twenty-four hours later, I read the message I was going to send, and was struck by the angry, accusatory words in it. I rewrote my message, modifying half its content and deleting the other half, then sent it. I got a shy reply and an apology from the other person."

## What should I do?

This week, whenever something happens that worries, scares or saddens you, accept your feelings. Don't reject these feelings or ignore them. Discuss them.

Share them with a friend.
Be sad.
Write them on a piece of paper, then tear it up.
Pray to God.
Put off your answer.
Act positive.

When you accept your feelings and deal with them, their load will lessen.

### Scientific study:

A study by Dr Wegner in 1994 confirmed that when we try to suppress some of our feelings, their influence only grows stronger.

Study name: "Ironic Processing".

## What should I read?

*Feel the Fear and Do It Anyway* by Susan Jeffers.

# HAPPINESS

6. Happiness Starts with Us
7. What Is Happiness?
8. You Can't Stop the Waves, but You Can Learn to Swim…
9. Unhappy Thoughts, Happy Thoughts…
10. What Makes You Happy Might Make Me Sad…
11. Why Do I Want to Be Happy?

# Happiness Starts with Us

You have many reasons to be happy. You also have many reasons to be sad. Happiness is your choice. Make yourself happy, for happiness starts with your choice.

**That's what happened**
The story revolves around a farmer, who was happy in his farm and successful at his job. He worked the land with diligence and vitality until he got older. One day, the farmer heard about people who travelled in search of diamonds, and how those who found them became very rich. Seduced by greed, the farmer got carried away, until his negative thoughts and comparisons got the better of him. Forgetting his happiness, he sold his land and set out to look for diamonds. He spent the next six months searching for them but his attempts were fruitless. He spent all the money he had made selling the farm, without finding anything! Unable to achieve his dream, he was overcome with hopelessness. Shortly afterwards he died, sad and heartbroken. Meanwhile, the new farmer who had bought our friend's land started working in the field with diligence and vitality, removing harmful weeds and planting new trees. Within a short time the land became one of the most prolific in the region. One day, while working, he found a shiny object. When he picked it up, it turned out to be a small diamond! He got very excited

and started digging and excavating, so he found a second, then a third… Surprise! He discovered a diamond mine beneath the land.

It's an old story but it makes many good points. The happiness we're looking for is often right where we are, beneath our feet; but we lose sight of it because of our preoccupation with other people's possessions! When you're looking for happiness, don't ignore the possibility that it's right where you are. Indeed, some of us want what others have, when all you need to do is think about what you have. Really, happiness is within your reach. It's in your inner field. If you tend to it and cultivate it, you will reap happiness and success (the diamonds). But if don't take care of it and water it, it will be invaded by harmful weeds (negative thoughts and habits) that will negatively impact your happiness and lifestyle.

# What Is Happiness?

Everyone in the world – whether Arabs or foreigners, rich or poor, young or old – has one thing in common. What you, I, and everyone else have in common is: we all want to be happy.

***Happiness is everyone's wish. Those who wish for money, rank or power, do so to be happy.***

If I asked you, or anyone else, "What do you want?" You would directly answer, "I want to be happy." Even if this isn't your answer, every wish people make, they make believing it will lead to happiness.

So, what is this happiness that everyone spends their time, money and efforts on?

The definitions of happiness vary. There are those who call it contentment, or obedience to the Merciful, or even pleasure. Others equate it with health, inner peace, or the fulfilment of life goals. Each of these definitions constitutes one aspect of happiness. For instance, contentment alone isn't considered happiness, since a lot of homeless people and prisoners consider themselves content with their life, but such a life is surely not an inspirational, happy one!

**A broader definition of happiness**
Positive feelings: the joy, cheerfulness, comfort, peace

of mind, contentment that you feel when you set out to accomplish your life goals with the right mindset (way of thinking) – whether you're a father, an employee, a businessman or a student. This also extend to your relationships with God and your friends, as well as all other aspects of your life.

Indeed, positive feelings without a goal are temporary and barely contribute to your happiness. An unsatisfying goal means you're not living the life you want, nor accomplishing your true goals in life.

> ***So, if you're successful in life, it doesn't mean that you're happy. Whereas if you are happy, it means you're successful in life.***

Reaching a goal with the wrong mindset is a mistake that won't make you happy. If you accomplish all your goals with a pessimistic mindset, you won't be happy. You won't be satisfied with what you have accomplished and you will live in anticipation of losing what you gained. Happiness starts within yourself.

If you're successful in life, it doesn't mean you're happy. Whereas if you are happy, it means you're successful in life. Studies indicate that happy people have a high problem-solving capacity. They are also more creative and more successful in their relationships.

# You Can't Stop the Waves, but You Can Learn to Swim

**50% innate nature + 10% life circumstances + 40% our choices, our thoughts = ☺**

Happiness is a mystery to most people. Hence, there is a common belief that happiness is an inborn trait or acquired by some thanks to their financial, cultural, or social circumstances, as well as joyous life events. This isn't true. Happiness isn't measured by what happens to us but by our reaction to it. For example, someone who just got fired from his job might decide to be miserable and blame society, while someone else might decide to look for a new job, thus discovering a different, more prosperous life with better conditions. Both faced the same situation but their reactions differed, so the results did too.

Leading a happy life isn't an easy feat; it may even be one of life's biggest challenges.

When faced with harsh circumstances, adversity, rejection and negative attitudes from others, it becomes difficult to own up to them, to pray to God and have confidence and composure. But one of the most important rules of happiness is knowing that we're in charge of our happiness, as well as our positive and negative decisions. Nothing, no one, can force us to think in a certain way without our consent. In a famous study that we will discuss later, it was proved that our happiness depends in large part on our thoughts and decisions rather than the circumstances we face. It doesn't mean that circumstances don't affect our happiness; but their influence remains limited, compared to that of our decisions. Indeed, we can't control our life circumstances but we can control our thoughts and decisions, and what we do about those circumstances. You can't stop the waves, but you can learn to swim. Still, we give up our power and exhaust ourselves with draining thoughts. In doing so, we forget the beautiful things and positive events, the praise we received and our accomplishments. Our thoughts are consumed by negative words and people, by mistakes we made and things we didn't accomplish. That is why we must always recall that we are in charge of our thoughts, behaviour and decisions; our life, our happiness.

It's important to realize that not everything we wish for will come true, and that things can't always go our way. Don't set preconditions for your happiness. Let happiness be a path you follow in life, with its ups and downs. Happiness is a decision we make. Some people spend their life waiting for happiness like you would wait for a taxi; or they think that there will come a day when happiness rains down on them. And so, they spend their life waiting for that happiness to come. We tie our happiness to outside circumstances, and this is the illusion that creates unhappiness! You can spend your whole life looking for false happiness in other places, while in truth, happiness is right in front of you.

An Indian sage said to one of his students, who was tired of searching for happiness, "I will tell you a secret: If you want to be happy, then be happy."

You are the centre of your own happiness. Everyone is searching for happiness, but the ignorant look for it in faraway places, whereas the wise plant happiness at their feet.

# Unhappy Thoughts, Happy Thoughts

**Unhappy thoughts**
Let us rid ourselves of wrong beliefs that negatively impact our happiness, such as:

My mood is ruining my life.

I could never be happy.

You're the reason for my misfortune.

My boss is ruining my life.

My life would get better if I moved to a new place.

My car, my house, this or that person, are the reason for my misery…

**Happy thoughts**
I'm in control of my happiness.

I choose happy thoughts.

My happiness doesn't depend on what I own or don't own. My happiness depends upon my contentment.

I let go of negative feelings with ease.

I can be increasingly happier with my life, regardless of my circumstances.

No one disturbs my mood without my permission.

My happiness doesn't depend on anyone else's happiness or unhappiness.

# What Makes You Happy Might Make Me Sad!

I visited a friend of mine at the farm owned by his father, a farmer from a young age, and we had a lovely, friendly visit. They threw a delicious dinner in my honour, then we had a pleasant conversation, during which my friend's father told me, "Did you know that I haven't left this farm in 50 years?! I am happy working here from dusk till dawn. Sometimes while praying, I even think about the number of palm trees, the time of harvest, the sheep and their babies, and how to organize them." Upon hearing this, my friend couldn't contain himself. With a sly smile, he said, "Forgive my honesty, Father, but my happiness started when I left the farm to go work in Jubail!"

***What makes this person happy might not apply to you, since God created every human on this earth for a purpose that fits him and satisfies his soul.***

Happiness is relative and each heart has its own set of happiness keys. So don't compare yourself to other people, nor your life to that of others; be it friends, relatives, or even the rich and famous. What makes other people happy might not apply to you, since God created every human on this earth for a purpose that fits him and satisfies his soul and which might not suit another.

Some find happiness at work or school, others in their relationships. There are those who find happiness in money, in learning, or giving, or in power. Happiness is relative and it mostly depends on you. Don't let your thoughts stray to others; don't wish for what they have in order to be happy. That would destroy your happiness. You don't know whether what they have will make you happy or miserable. Have a positive outlook on what others possess, wish them well and never envy them. Envy should be reserved for people who spend their money charitably, or impart their wisdom on others. As for everything else, simply disregard it. One study states that when basic needs – food, shelter, minimum wage – are met, money becomes an insignificant factor in increasing happiness, well behind other reasons related to your personality and goals.

A person with limited income thinks that bliss is tied to money which, as we mentioned, is simply not true. With each passing day, we are more and more certain that the traditional notions of happiness – fame, power and money – are unrealistic, and mostly unrelated to real happiness. Indeed, many rich people are miserable! Many celebrities and actors commit suicide, and many well-known office holders lead unhappy lives!

A study was conducted on a group of people who moved from a noisy city to a beautiful village with a peaceful atmosphere. At first, their happiness levels increased significantly, but three months later, those levels had returned to what they were before the move. This only confirms that happiness mainly depends on you.

# Why Do I Want to Be Happy?

With hundreds of studies on the subject, the benefits of happiness are no longer in doubt. Indeed, a happy person:
- is more successful at his job
- lives comfortably and blissfully with his family
- has many friends, and happy relationships
- is healthier, with a stronger immune system; he also lives longer and is less prone to heart disease and strokes
- has a more balanced personality
- is highly resilient in the face of shocking events and problems

Let's go through some interesting studies on happiness:

**The flu virus study**

A group of people volunteered for a research aiming to study the effects of the flu on them. First, their happiness level was measured. Then they were all exposed to the flu virus. The researchers put these people up in a hotel for 5 days, then continued monitoring them for a month. Once the results were out, they showed that the happiest people were the least affected by the virus; which confirms that happiness positively impacts a person's immune system. This applies to all of us: when a person goes through periods of sadness and pain, he is more frequently sick and tired.

The toxins produced by the constant sense of fear, anger and frustration destroy our health. Therefore, you can't lead an angry, hateful life, and still be healthy, since your physical health is a reflection of your mental health. When you strive to make yourself or your parents happy, cheer them up, bring joy to their life and rid them of negativity, God willing, you protect them from diseases and increase their strength. Keep in mind that your happiness and good health are your birthright. Be gentle with yourself and work hard to make yourself happy, as well as those around you, without feeling guilty or selfish; people close to you will share your happiness.

## Happiness increases your chances of success and a distinguished career

In another study, researchers paid a visit to a government facility, where they measured the happiness levels of the employees. They visited the same facility again three and a half years later. This time, they asked the managers of that facility to evaluate several aspects of the employees' performance, such as:

Do they suggest good, useful business ideas?

Do they have clear goals?

Do they have good communication skills? Good listening skills?

Do they work efficiently with their colleagues? Are they good at teamwork?

The happiest people had an outstanding score in every category, and they were more productive, effective and distinguished in their work.

## Happiness strengthens your relationships

In a study conducted on children in Year 5, researchers guided a number of pupils through an exercise that triggers happiness, called "benevolence to others". The pupils were asked to do three good deeds, even simple ones: helping their mother, welcoming their father, cleaning a room at home, giving alms. Weeks later, upon measuring the students' happiness levels, the researchers noticed an increase in them. Then they polled all the students in that class to identify the ones who everyone prefers to sit and talk with. The happiest students turned out to be the most popular among their classmates; which is an obvious and intuitive result, since we all love to sit with people who make us happy and comfortable.

### WHAT SHOULD I DO?

Test yourself to find out your happiness level. This is an easy way to measure how happy you are. Fill in the following table with a number from 1 to 10; 1 being extremely unhappy and 10 extremely happy.

| Area of life | My degree of happiness |
| --- | --- |
| My family life (my immediate family) | |
| My relationships (my relatives) | |
| My relationships (my friends) | |
| My job | |
| My health | |
| My relationship with God | |

Add the numbers, then divide them by 5, and you will get your happiness level.
- Less than 5: Unhappy
- 5-6: Average happiness, like most people
- 6-8: Happy
- Higher than 8: Extremely happy

**Scientific study:**

The study "The How of Happiness" 50% 40% 10%, conducted by Professor Sonja Lyubomirsky.

**What should I read?**

The book *Being Happy!* by Andrew Matthews.

# YOUR HAPPINESS IS UNDER YOUR CONTROL

12. Your Thoughts Determine Your Quality of Life
13. You Control 40%
14. From 40% to 100%!

# Your Thoughts Determine Your Quality of Life

A lot of people who have it worse than you are still happy; and a lot of people who have it better than you are still miserable! Happiness is your decision.

**That's what happened**
The husband sat at his desk, grabbed a pen, and wrote:

"In the past year, I had a gallbladder removal surgery and was bedridden for months. I turned 60 and left an important position at the publishing house where I worked for 30 years. My father passed away. My son failed in medical school, having missed months of studying after his injury in a car accident."

And at the bottom of the page, he wrote: "What a very bad year!!"

His wife came into the room and saw him lost in thought. So she got close to him, and looking over his shoulder, read what he had written. Then she quietly left the room without a word.

A few minutes later, she came back with a piece of paper in hand, which she calmly placed next to the paper her husband wrote. The husband picked his wife's paper and started reading:

"In the past year, you got rid of your gallbladder pains, which had been tormenting you for years. You turned 60 and are in perfect health. You made a deal to publish more than one important book, which allowed you to dedicate yourself to writing. Your father lived to be 85 years old without ever causing any trouble and died peacefully, without suffering. Your son escaped death in a car accident and recovered without any impairments or complications…"

The wife ended her letter by writing: "What a year God blessed us with; and we got through it in one piece!"

The same events, but with a different perspective… Events aren't the only thing that affects your happiness. Your way of dealing with them, your actions and your thoughts, are also a factor in your happiness or unhappiness. Unhappy people blame their circumstances. Happy people transcend these circumstances and view every obstacle as a challenge they need to overcome and learn from. To them, life is a series of fortunate events or valuable lessons.

# You Control 40%

50% innate nature + 10% life circumstances + 40% our choices, our thoughts = ☺

Happiness is a mystery to most people. Hence, there is a common belief that happiness is innate, or acquired by some thanks to their financial, cultural, or social circumstances, as well as joyous life events. This isn't true. In a famous study conducted by Dr Sonja for 20 years, it was proven that happiness depends on three factors:

50% of our happiness is an inborn trait.

40% consist of our choices/thoughts/actions.

Only 10% depend on our circumstances, such as money, work or even our childhood.

In a study conducted on people who won huge cash prizes, it was found that their happiness levels increased significantly for six months. But then they returned to the same levels as before their big win.

If you're dreaming of getting into a certain college, or getting a certain job, and your dream comes true, then your happiness levels will undoubtedly increase. But a few months later, your level of happiness will return to its previous state.

When you lose money, or a loved one, you will be sad. But after a while, most of these feelings will go away and you will return to normal.

Some even think that living in a country like the USA, or in a certain city, will make them happy. That's not true. People who live there have virtually the same happiness levels as others elsewhere; so long as the city in question isn't plagued by poverty, famine or war. Of course, when we move to a new place, sometimes we feel our happiness level rise; but shortly thereafter, it goes back down.

*If you only change outside circumstances without changing your inner self, it wouldn't affect more than 10% of your happiness.*

It would be wrong to think that changing external circumstances would make us happier. If you only change outside circumstances without changing your inner self, it wouldn't affect more than 10% of your happiness.

Keep in mind that our actions account for 40% of our happiness, which is four times the amount of influence our circumstances – which we may or may not control – have. We might not be able to control our life circumstances, but we can control our thoughts and decisions, and what we do about those circumstances. And that constitutes 40% of our happiness.

*Your decisions, deeds and thoughts either raise or lower your happiness.*
*And you are the one who picks and chooses.*

What determines our happiness or unhappiness isn't the circumstances we go through. Rather, it is the way we go about our daily life. Everything you do or don't do can either raise or lower your happiness levels. Your income could increase or decrease. Still, you choose whether you want to get an education; whether you want to forgive, or hold a grudge. You choose to visit a relative or a friend; to return a favour; to ignore what a foolish stranger did in the street; to let go of a painful past and move forward with your life. Happiness is about our way of thinking and interpreting events, and what we decide to focus on. All these decisions, deeds and thoughts either raise or lower your happiness. And you are the one who picks and chooses.

One day, two friends went to the bank to take out a loan for 180 thousand dirhams each. One of them decided to buy a Mercedes, while the other thought, "Why am I spending debt money on something perishable?" So he decided to buy three plots of land. Four years later, their value multiplied to over one million dirhams. Then he began to build a career, until he became Ahmed Al Abdulla, the owner of New Dubai Properties, and one of the richest people in the UAE. They both took out the same loan but their decisions differed, and so did the results. Ahmed was not content with the change that happened to him. He sought to make his own change in order to become happier; to spread happiness around him, with his company supporting social initiatives. Moreover, he puts a positive spin on events and situations, like, for instance, considering a failure as an edifying experience; or focusing on what he gained instead of what he lost. He also believes that his experience is a common right from which everyone can learn.

***There is certainly a difference in thoughts, behaviour and everyday life of the happy and the unhappy, the successful and the unsuccessful.***

There is certainly a difference in thoughts, behaviour and everyday life of the happy and the unhappy, the successful and the unsuccessful. Happiness can be taught. It isn't a secret anymore, since the modern world has revealed all the factors that influence a person's happiness or misery. Unhappy people can easily be taught happy habits and the way to incorporate them, which improves their lives. This serves to show that you are in control of your happiness; not your neighbour, your boss, your husband or your financial situation. These are – as we have seen – circumstances that only constitute 10% of our happiness.

# From 40% to 100%!

As we now know, 40% of our happiness is under our control. However, 50%–which is a very high percentage–is in our innate nature; meaning it's in our genes. We can all surely think of some people we know who exude happiness as if they were born with it! They're optimistic, joyous, pleasant, because they were given the whole 50%. Plus, they strived to improve their lives, making the right decisions that lead to happiness. And so, they lead an enjoyable, beautiful life.

You might find this fact depressing, but then you would be thinking like everyone else!

"What if I was unlucky and only got 10% instead of 50%?"

"What a pity! This means that no matter what I do, my happiness level will never exceed 50%! O God, how is this fair?!"

***Yes, you can increase the 40% happiness that you control to reach 100%.***

I am telling you that God is wise and wouldn't wrong so much as an atom. He created everything exactly as it should be. He gave every person what suits him and makes him happy – if he is satisfied and does what he can with what God gave him.

But you might wonder, "How so, when God only gave me 20% of happiness at birth?"

Yes, you can increase the 40% happiness that you control to reach 100%.

This statement isn't based on delusions or false hope; it's a scientific fact. Indeed, scientists have made a discovery called "epigenetics", or gene remodelling; meaning that the way you think and deal with your feelings, and with others, affects your genes and brain cells.

***When you focus on the negative aspects of your life, and look for sad events, and let the most trivial situations get to you; you program your genes negatively.***

When you decide to get over past negative situations, and other people's wrongdoings and words; when you are keen on giving, and accept what you can't control; when you stay away from what bothers you, doing what you love instead; when you forgive and decide to focus on what makes you happy, then you would be reprogramming your genes to increase your chances of happiness. Whereas when you focus on the negative aspects of your life, and look for sad events, and let the most trivial situations get to you; when you live in fear of the future, and focus on the things you don't have:

"I'm not married. I don't own a house. My job is exhausting. I don't have any relationships. What did he mean by what he said…"

Thus, you programme your genes negatively, so even if you were born with happiness genes, you would be stopping them from working, and reducing their impact!

But there are many seeds of happiness and success that God hid in your genes: ideas, innovations, good relationships, success in business, promotions. When you do the best you can in life, nothing will stop good things from reaching you – neither envious people nor bad circumstances; neither your university tutor, nor your boss at work, nor any temporary loss.

For God doesn't let hard work go to waste, and doesn't destroy hope.

The bottom line is, if we manage our lives well, and do the best we can with the 40% we control, we will take control of the 50% that we were born with. We will then reprogram those 50% in favour of our happiness.

That is why your happiness depends solely on you.

If you can change the way you think, your mind will change.

And if you can change your choices and actions, your life will change.

#### What should I do?
I will reprogramme my convictions for the better. Every morning, I will decide:

That my day will be happy and that I will be satisfied with whatever happens that day.

I believe that my thoughts, choices and actions make or break my happiness.

I choose to live the days to come with joy and delight.

### Scientific study:
The study "The How of Happiness" 50% 40% 10%, conducted by Professor Sonja Lyubomirsky.

#### What should I read?
*The Habit of Winning* by Prakash Iyer: A book containing a number of inspiring stories, about people who didn't succumb to destructive circumstances or thoughts.

# YOUR CIRCUMSTANCES, A CROSSROADS, AND YOUR CHOICE

15. Problems and Misfortunes Can Be Motivating
16. Psychological Flexibility Lays the Foundation for Your Strength and Personality
17. The Way We Handle a Problem Affects Our Health and Our Life
18. The Most Flexible Trees
19. Your Treasure Is Hidden Under Your Rock
20. Flexibility Improves your Strength and Your Personality

# Problems and Misfortunes Can Be Motivating

Problems either hinder us or increase our abilities. Depending on how you look at a problem, it can hinder you or increase your ability, so that you not only overcome it but become a better person.

**That's what happened**
An area with poor living conditions became known for the number of students abandoning their studies and turning to a life of crime and violence. So the country's government asked a group of psychologists to study this phenomenon in the area. The researchers tried to solve the following mysteries:

Why are big numbers of students in that area running away? Why is violence spreading there?

Why are a lot of the area's youths failing?

The intensive study lasted ten years and cost the government a lot of money to cover the expenses generated by the specialists' great efforts. But in the end, it didn't yield any results; the situation improved slightly, but the problem was never solved. The researchers had made the following suggestions: a better education system, better school buildings. The situation remained the same until 1980, when another scientist came along, with a different approach than his predecessors. So, instead of asking, "Why are these students failing?" he asked a different question, "Why are some students succeeding despite their difficult circumstances?!"

This was of thinking was the main reason for the researchers' success, having thus learned these students' secret – the secret behind their ability to overcome obstacles that a lot of their friends couldn't. The big secret that these researchers uncovered is flexibility in the face of problems, hardships and obstacles.

# Psychological Flexibility Lays the Foundation for Your Strength and Personality

All of our lives are filled with events that could potentially destroy our happiness. We all face disappointments and afflictions. You could receive unexpected bad news about your health or ruin your relationship with a loved one; you could realize that a dream of yours is dead or fail to achieve something you put your mind to.

It's very easy to be depressed and weak, and lose your appetite for life. But if we want to see God's gifts and blessings, we must be flexible; which means that:

➤ When we trip and fall, we don't stay down. We get back up and try again. More precisely, we try new ways, since what we were doing clearly wasn't working. And we know that there is no obstacle too hard to overcome, no dilemma that can't be solved, no sickness we can't recover from. No one can destroy our life, and nothing can prevent what God has intended for us

➤ When something upsetting happens, or when we don't get what we wanted, we don't get angry and complain, blaming others and lamenting our luck. Instead, we think positive, as we know that what befell us couldn't have been prevented. We also know that God always works for our own good, even if we can't see it at that moment. And so, we carry on with our life, feeling better than before

### *He who possesses psychological flexibility can keep calm in the face of difficulties.*

Your ability to persevere and show positive growth in the face of pressures and afflictions determines not only your level of flexibility, but also your happiness and success in life.

Psychological flexibility determines two important elements for your happiness and success in life:
- Your ability to keep trying, and not give up prematurely when something doesn't go your way.
- Your ability to return to normal after going through a crisis; and even be in a better state than before.

Psychological flexibility can explain why some people can keep calm in the face of difficulties, while others who encounter the same obstacle suffer a complete breakdown. It's because flexible people have the ability to use their skills and strengths to meet problems and challenges, and recover from them. Moreover, they do so regardless of the nature of those problems – trouble at work, financial problems, sickness, a divorce, the loss of a loved one…

In contrast, every person who isn't equipped with this flexibility becomes vulnerable to circumstances that could destroy his life and make it intolerable.

# The Way We Handle a Problem Impacts Our Health and Our Life

No obstacles can stand in the face of your perseverance; for the gates of knowledge and wisdom are always open to all. So know that no matter what life throws your way, it will give you experience, and motivate you to let go of your past – whatever it may be – and move towards a brighter future.

***You will encounter problems and difficulties, which you can overcome and even turn into blessings, if you are flexible.***

Don't let despair seep into you. Have an open mind; think and consult others; use all the methods that can benefit you. Thus, your ability to overcome difficulties and solve problems will increase. And remember that you are only human, you are constantly learning and will continue to do so. Love life, and you will find the best in it.

Yes, you will encounter problems and difficulties; so be flexible in order to overcome these obstacles and turn them into blessings. Always strive to better yourself, to become stronger and more solid and lead a happy life. Because if you don't, you will fall into the trap of misery. And remember, no one else but you is responsible for your own happiness.

Also, recall the story of the man whose car broke down in Riyadh at midnight. He looked for someone to give him a hand, but couldn't find anyone to help. He ended up wasting six hours and paying double for his car repairs. This could happen to anyone and it could upset them and ruin their day. But Salman Al-Suhaibaney decided to turn this problem into a gift, and look for a way out. Indeed, he decided to develop a platform for roadside assistance, "Morni", which became a huge success, with over 500 thousand users. He also set up a fleet for urgent car maintenance.

When you're flexible, you learn that:
➤ Every problem, misfortune, or disaster is temporary and will not last forever. Therefore, I will not spend my day upset and resentful, thinking about my bad situation, money, loss and missed opportunities. Rather, I know that God will compensate me for my loss and grant me something better than what my unfulfilled wish. Hence, I will become stronger, healthier and better than before (Indeed, the patient will be given their reward), and say: Between the blink of an eye and its attention. God changes from state to state.
➤ The way we respond to adversity has an impact on our life, health, and progress.

In a study at the University of Chicago, conducted by Dr Salvatore R. Maddi on 25,000 recently fired individuals:
➤ A third had different kinds of breakdown; some of them had heart attacks, some suffered from

anxiety and depression, and others worsening family problems, divorce and violence
- A third were flexible; which made them overcome these problems and find jobs elsewhere, thus improving their lives

# The Most Flexible Trees

A specialist passed through an area that was hit by a devastating hurricane and saw vast surfaces destroyed, with a large number of fallen trees: huge oak trees, sixty-foot-tall cypress trees, hard-trunked tamarisk, eucalyptus and cedar trees. All cut down, destroyed by tornadoes moving at 120 miles per hour. However, there was one kind of tree that was still standing, which the strong winds were unable to break or destroy. This tree was none other than the palm tree; but why? What is this tree's secret to surviving the hurricane?!

God created the palm tree to withstand the winds.

One peculiar study showed that palm trees have a strange structure. Thanks to it, they can resist the strongest of winds, unlike other trees.

➤ Thanks to its high flexibility, the palm tree can bend without breaking; to the point that its top can touch the ground without its trunk breaking. And once the storm passes, its trunk is so flexible that it recovers its normal shape

➤ When strong winds hit the palm tree, its roots adapt to them, by growing to give the tree extra resistance. After a hurricane hits, the palm tree doesn't just go back to its previous shape; it becomes stronger than before

You should have the flexibility of a palm tree. In fact, the Prophet himself (peace be upon him) talked about it.

## THE MOST FLEXIBLE TREES

"A believer is like the tree that does not lose a single tip; do you know which one?" They said, "No." He said, "The palm tree, which does not lose a single tip. Similarly, not a single prayer of a believer will be lost."

Every tornado that you encounter in life may bend and hurt you, but you have enough flexibility not to allow it to take away your smile and not to let it break you. You can stumble but you don't stay down. You can suffer from a betrayal or the loss of a loved one, an unfulfilled wish or a health scare. But you don't break. Instead, you turn to God and put your trust in Him. So you recover and get back to your normal life; not as you were, but stronger, happier, better. Thus is the flexibility of a believer; he doesn't let life's pitfalls make him miserable, nor does he despair in the face of difficulties.

**Happy thoughts:**
- Flexibility is the key to success; if what you're doing isn't working, change your method. There is always a better way and you will surely see better results
- You should combine flexibility and firmness: be firm, so you don't give up on your goal; and be flexible, so you adapt to circumstances, avoid obstacles and turn them to your advantage when necessary
- The more flexible person is in control of any given situation
- Positivity doesn't mean never having any problems. Rather, it's about flexible thinking; accepting your circumstances and adapting them to achieve your goal.
- Don't be so strict that circumstances break you, nor so soft that the slightest change bends you. Be

flexible. Flexibility is the art of handling life with the least trouble and the most benefit

### What should I do?
Personal training:
- ➤ Think of a problem you're currently facing
- ➤ Define the problem in clear and simple words
- ➤ Find out the roots and causes of the problem
- ➤ Make a quick list of solutions
- ➤ Be positive and look for opportunities
- ➤ Consult a friend, then compare his opinion with your solutions
- ➤ Apply the solution that you both agree or converge on, then go over the benefits

**Scientific study:**
"Learning from Flexibility", a study by researcher Amy Warner.

### What should I read?
*Faraj Ba'd al-Shiddah*, by Judge Al Tanukhi.
*13 Things Mentally Strong People Don't Do*, by Amy Morin.

# Your Treasure Is Hidden Under Your Rock

Problems either hinder us or enhance our abilities. Depending on how you view a problem, it can hinder you or it can enhance your abilities, so that you not only overcome it but also become a better person.

**That's what happened**
There once was a king who wanted to teach his people an important lesson. So, he put a huge rock in the middle of a road, blocking it, and hid a treasure and a note under it. Then he hid to watch his subjects' reactions.

How will a passer-by react to the rock? Will he try to remove it, get help, use some tools and tricks, or give up and turn back?

The king watched the road, and saw frustration and despair. Some people didn't do anything but most of them gave up after one try.

A while later, a farmer came along. He contemplated the rock, before trying time and again to move it; but he couldn't. Then, he had an idea. He brought a tree trunk and used it to push the rock from a certain angle. Indeed, his idea worked. and he moved the rock. To his surprise, he found the treasure and a piece of paper that read:

"Our path in life is filled with obstacles, but each obstacle you encounter will either strengthen or weaken you, depending on your reaction."

As long as we're still breathing, we will keep facing obstacles; that's life. An obstacle can turn into an opportunity or a crisis, however. Whether you're looking for a job or are already employed; whether you're in a bad relationship or are having money trouble; whether you're a student or trying to accomplish something, you will encounter obstacles. What's important is knowing that there's a way to work with them. The biggest obstacle you can face is not the obstacle itself but the way you deal with it. When faced with a hurdle, some just suffer and give up, while others are flexible enough to try, experiment, suffer, learn and become better. Inflexibility may be the worst enemy of happiness.

When we allow circumstances, people and obstacles to bring us down, we enter a vicious circle of weakness, surrender and misery that is hard to get out of. But when we see ourselves try and experiment; when we see that we're capable of overcoming obstacles and are fit to deal with problems and difficulties, we stop feeling frustrated. Instead, we feel powerful; that is the path to happiness.

# Flexibility Improves Your Strength and Your Personality

**Path to flexibility**
Trust in God ⟶ Believe in yourself ⟶ Rely on others ⟶ Remember your idols ⟶ Nurture positive feelings ⟶ Your way of thinking ⟶ Give yourself hope

**Trust in God:** You may stumble, you may fail, you may fall ill and you may lose what you love but you never know; perhaps God is trying to protect you and keep you from harm. Take the person who was walking in the street and had a sudden, painful fall. He thus avoided getting run over by a speeding car that would have killed him! Or listen to Umm Salma, who recalls: "When my husband died, I told God: 'God, reward me in my plight, and send someone better my way.' Then I came to my senses and said: 'How could I find anyone better than Abu Salma?' But, at the end of my Iddah, the Prophet himself took me as his wife; God had indeed given me someone better." Trust in God, for He will always give you better than you have already and He will grant you better things than you lost. If you lose a loved one, He will compensate you for your loss; if you fall ill, God is healing and giving, and has power over all things.

***Self-flagellation will make your life a difficult and painful experience that is not subject to progress or change.***

**Believe in yourself:** Self-confidence plays a prominent role in overcoming obstacles, dealing with stress and recovering from traumatic events. When you're feeling depressed or weak, remind yourself of your strengths and accomplishments. Increasing your confidence in your ability to respond and deal with a crisis builds flexibility. Trust that you are a great person and don't bring yourself down; that wouldn't improve your life. Self-flagellation will make your life a difficult and painful experience that is not subject to progress or change. Remember that self-love unleashes your talents and unlocks your potential.

**Rely on others:** Isolation wreaks havoc on your nervous system. Furthermore, some obstacles can't be overcome alone; you need to share some burdens with others to lighten their load. No man is an island. Everyone needs someone; that is a fact of life. The mere presence of other people by your side, sharing your feelings and giving you advice, offers you protection during hard times. It's important for you to have someone you can trust and talk to, as it allows you to express your feelings and get the right support, effective help and possible solutions. It also enhances your flexibility. Don't face your problems alone. True, a problem might seem too big to solve but when you share it, you get a different perspective and find solutions. Using your mind to consult with others is an art form. According to one study, sharing your problems with someone you trust reduces anxiety by

55%. Sometimes, charity can be an important means to get through a rough patch. Indeed, you help yourself by helping others; because it brings you comfort and strength, in addition to releasing dopamine – the happy hormone.

*There's nothing more beautiful than learning about other people's life experience; when you face difficulties, remember those who came before you.*

**Remember your idols:** The biographies of the great and the successful are an inspiration. They offer entertainment, action, as well as the gist of these people's life experience – how they lived, how flexible they were in the face of the obstacles and difficulties they encountered on their path. There's nothing more beautiful than learning about other people's life experience; when you face difficulties, remember those who came before you.

The poor, the orphans, the immigrants, the expelled, the oppressed. Some came from nothing and others faced horrible circumstances. Nevertheless, they considered it a challenge and went through the experience. They moved past their flaws and circumstances and put up with abuse, viewing each problem as an obstacle to overcome. Who are your idols? It doesn't have to be someone who passed away 500 years ago; they could still be alive. For instance, Sultan Al-Athel can only move his eyelids, and he still manages ten thousand employees! Mustafa Sadiq al-Rafi'i did miracles for Arabic literature despite a typhoid fever destroying his hearing and his body; and Stephen Hawking, the greatest physicist of the modern age, could only move his eyelids. It doesn't even need to be someone famous. A distinguished architect I know told me that his idol is his son, who was born with one arm. His boy inspires him every day, each time he sees him solve a problem or get over a difficulty. It might seem easy to us, but in his condition, it's hard. Think of those around you: your father, your mother, your friend…

So who's your idol, the one you'll remember when the going gets tough?

***Everybody gets scared when faced with unusual circumstances.***

**Nurture positive feelings:** God, in His wisdom, created negative feelings like fear and sadness to help us when we need it. Indeed, sadness during a tragedy is beneficial; so is fear in the face of danger, as it makes us avoid it. Everybody gets scared when faced with unusual circumstances. Our Prophet Ibrahim's heart was filled with fear, as was Musa's. But these feelings weren't made to last longer than intended, because then they would take over your life, stop you in your tracks and destroy your will. Conversely, positive feelings will make you feel safe and comfortable. And when you feel safe, you become more open, creative, receptive and understanding. You're also more determined in the face of difficulties and problems; and that means you're more flexible. A study further confirmed that positive feelings give us strength in the present, and improve our health and personality in the future. As a matter of fact, gratitude, contentment, joyfulness, hope, love and other positive feelings strengthen our flexibility.

**The way you think:** Sometimes, it's not what happens that affects us, but rather how we respond to it. Depending on our way of thinking, the same event can be perceived differently, and its effects can vary. Where one person sees an opportunity, another sees a threat. What someone views as a cooperation, someone else views as a competition; what someone sees as entertaining can seem like a routine, boring task for others; and what someone considers a tragedy, another sees as a noble test.

A negative person thinks he's the problem and the reason behind a failure. Whereas a flexible person rationally examines the reason… So even if he is part of it, he looks for a solution rather than focusing on the problem.

A negative person also thinks that problems will last forever and ever. Whereas for a flexible person, problems are temporary and unavoidable. Will they end today, tomorrow? Only God knows. But they will end. Furthermore, a negative person carries his problems over to other aspects of his life, so the slightest bump in the road ruins his day and controls his life. Whereas a flexible person knows the extent and repercussions of a problem, without blowing them out of proportion.

That is why your way of thinking determines what you get out of life. It can fuel your will to achieve your goals and persevere, so you keep getting better.

Religious people are at the highest levels of flexibility. In good times, they are grateful to God, which does them good; in bad times, they are patient, which also does them good. They have no room for generalizations, self-blame or despair of God's mercy; a sign of flexibility at its best!

A friend of mine, Dr Khaled Al Harthi, CEO of a media production company, once told me: "We went through a crisis in the year 1436 AH that almost cost us the company. This financial crisis was due to the government's budget cuts, and most of our contracts were with government agencies. We decided not to surrender to reality and looked for ways to overcome the crisis instead of giving in to it. We ventured into e-commerce, and started creating apps, which preserved our standing. And we came back better than before." So you see, a crisis may be an opportunity, or it may be a fatal blow, depending on how you deal with it. As long as you don't give up, you're in a good position.

**Give yourself the power of hope:** It's hard to be optimistic when you're having problems or are in a tough situation. But optimism is an important part of being flexible, as well as a sign of trust in God. Take Yusuf (peace be upon him) for instance. He suffered from his brothers' hatred, was thrown down a well, then imprisoned. Still, he didn't lose hope; so God moved him to the king's castle in Egypt, where he became his minister. Optimism doesn't mean ignoring the issue, but that we understand what happened, have faith in God, believe that it will pass, and trust our skills and abilities in order to face and overcome challenges.

Optimism makes it easier to bear difficulties, and the belief that tomorrow will be better gives us the strength to overcome obstacles. In fact, studies have shown that a patient's optimism is a big factor in his recovery.

### What should I do?
Categorizing the problems and circumstances you're going through helps you solve them, since there are circumstances you can't control, others you can handle on your own and others still that require outside intervention. Organize your circumstances and difficulties in this way and when you accept what you can't change, you will get enough

comfort and strength to change what you can.

| My goal | Things I can't change | Changes I need others' help with | Things I can change on my own |
|---|---|---|---|
| Make my country better | The corruption of some officials | Improving the work environment | Developing myself in my field, learning and making plans for advancement |
| Provide my children with the best upbringing | Having bad pupils at my child's school | Spreading awareness about education and communicating with the school | Raising, educating and protecting my children |
| Go to university | Nepotism / Other people having connexions | Learning about different colleges, majors and admission requirements | Doing my best to get excellent grades |
| Improve my relationship with my wife | Sudden outbursts of anger for no reason | Learning about communication skills | Being friendly, changing gradually and accepting what I can't change |

## Scientific study:

"Psychological resilience and its relationship with satisfaction of life", Al-Azhar University.

"Positive Emotions Broaden and Build", a study by Barbara L. Fredrickson.

**WHAT SHOULD I READ?**
*The Obstacle Is the Way*, by Ryan Holiday.

# YOU ATTRACT WHAT YOU FOCUS ON

21. You Always Get More of What You Focus on
22. Your Focus Makes Your Happiness and Your Life
23. Reverse the Telescope
24. What You See Is What You Get
25. Happy thoughts

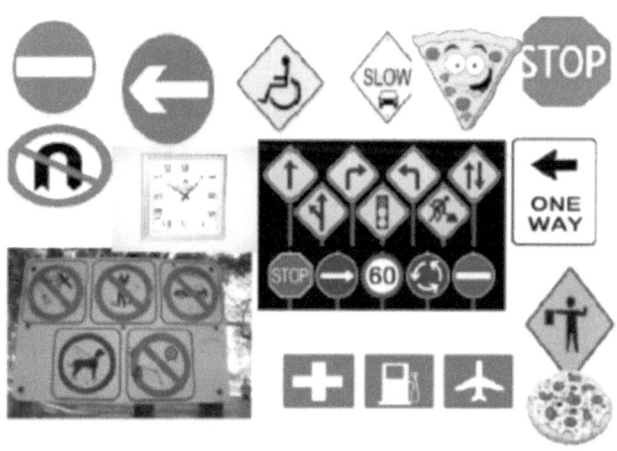

# You Always Get More of What You Focus on

When you focus on what you can't change, you drown in anger and sorrow. Instead, accept what you can't change and focus on what you can, and you will become more positive.

**The Challenge**

This challenge will illustrate an important idea. Focus on the image below for 10 seconds, trying to count the number of circular shapes.

Now that you're done, how many circular shapes did you find? 10, 20, 30?

Answer the next question without looking at the image. What time does the clock indicate?

If you didn't answer correctly, you're among the 98% who don't know the answer. But why? The reason is that you get what you focus on, and you're guided towards what you think of. Focus is a major strength but it can work to your advantage or disadvantage depending on how you use it. If you focus on your positive features and those of others, you will find a lot of them. Similarly, if you focus on the negative ones, they're all you will see. You are the one who creates your own reality!

# Your focus Makes Your Happiness and Your Life

Focus on your goals, not your problems. Focus on what you want rather than what you don't. Focus on God's blessings instead of what you lack. This is the essence of happiness: where do you place your awareness and what do you focus on?

If you only focus on your problems, you won't see any solutions.

If you only focus on what you don't want, you won't get what you do want.

If you only focus on what you lack, you won't enjoy the many blessings you already have.

***If you focus on problems, circumstances you're going through, obstacles and people who have wronged you, you would be robbing yourself of peace.***

What you focus on takes hold of you and your energy. If you focus on those who wronged you, you are letting them harm you over and over again. And if you focus on your painful past, you are bringing all the hurt back to the surface!

If you focus on problems, circumstances you're going through, obstacles, and people who have wronged you, they will invade your thoughts and upset you. You will then feel weak and lose the taste for anything good. Hence, the secret to overcoming these obstacles and enjoying life is to focus on your goals, your ambitions and the good things you have going.

I once went on a cruise to an island with some friends. After we boarded the ship, one friend noticed it was making an annoying sound. The rest of us got over this inconvenience. We decided to focus on the ride, the beautiful nature and the lovely atmosphere. But the friend in question didn't like this decision. He kept complaining about the ship, broken promises, false advertising and that annoying sound that ruined a lovely trip. In reality, the sound didn't ruin his trip; his decision to focus on that sound did. As for the rest of us, we had an extremely fun ride.

> ***If you focus on your goals, on what you can do, on the good things… you will be at peace and your life will improve.***

Consequently, when you focus on upsetting matters, no matter how trivial, they will grow in size and take over your thoughts. They will blind you to your goals and the good things in your life and cause you to behave in ways unbefitting of the life you want.

But, when you focus on your goals, on what you can do, on the good in others, you will notice them more. You will feel better and your relationships will improve, because you're only seeing the good in them.

# Reverse the Telescope

There's a story about a young boy who was afraid of his violent neighbour. The latter was the same age, but he was much larger. So this young boy was too scared to go out, because he didn't have the confidence to stand up to the gigantic boy.

One day, the father walked in on his son and found him looking at the street through a telescope. Oddly, the boy was looking through the other end of the telescope. And it's known that when you turn a telescope around, it makes things appear smaller rather than larger.

The father was taken aback by his son's strange behaviour and asked him about it; to which he replied, "I want to see this giant as a dwarf, so I won't be afraid of him. I want to think of him as small and worthless!"

You too need to reverse the telescope and change your focus on your problems, not exaggerating them or focusing on them too much. Turn the telescope around and look at the wonderful things in your life. Instead of being afraid and worried, know that God is bigger than all things. He will grant you what you desire and no matter how big your problems seem, they are infinitely small before His grace.

Take Sarah, Ibrahim's wife, for example. She was 99 years old when she found out she was pregnant. "How can I have a child when I'm old? How can I have a child when I'm sterile? How can I have a child when my husband is an old man!"

## REVERSE THE TELESCOPE

***If you focus on the difficulties,
on what you don't want and on negative things, you
will stray from your goals and dreams.***

How often do we exaggerate difficulties in our life? I can't have children. There's no way I'm recovering from this illness. I doubt that I'll get promoted. I will never own a house. I will never realize my wishes and dreams!

If you focus on the difficulties, on what you don't want and on negative things, you will make them bigger, and weaken your faith in God. You will also stray from your goals and dreams. Indeed, if you're broke and you focus on your bankruptcy, your poorness, your necessity, you will feel helpless and weak; because, as we have seen, negative feelings overpower our positive thinking and bring us down. If instead you focus on a clear goal, like making a specific amount of money in a specific amount of time; if you write down ideas that will help you reach your goal; and if, first and foremost, you rely on God and trust in Him, then you will reinforce your positive feelings, raise your self-confidence and widen your options. Thus you will be much closer to accomplishing your goal since, contrary to negative focus, which distracts and hinders you, positive focus helps you reach your goals.

Trust in God, focus on what you want and the blessings you have, and you will lead a happier life – no matter what people say, no matter how many weaknesses you have and no matter how many difficulties you face.

# What You See Is What You Get

A traveller was passing by a village, when he encountered an old man standing on the side of the road. So he stopped and asked him, "How are people's manners and behaviour in this village?"

The old man stood in thought, before answering, "And how were people's manners and behaviour in the village you came from?"

The traveller said, "The people were vile, ugly, spiteful, and hardly any of them smiled!"

So the man replied, "You will be treated the same way here you were treated there."

After the traveller left, another one stopped by and asked the same question, "How are people's manners and behaviour in this village?"

The old man answered, "And how were people's manners and behaviour in the village you came from?"

He answered, "The people were good, friendly, kind-hearted and well-mannered."

So the old man stated, "You will be treated the same way here you were treated there."

The idea expressed by the wise man is very important. It means that the way you see others affects the way you treat them and consequently, the way they treat you. If you see the good in them, overlooking their mistakes and their flaws, it will reflect on the way you treat them. Indeed, there's a famous saying that goes, "Judging others does not define who they are, it defines who you are."

**Pay attention to your focus:** the way you focus can make you happy or miserable. It can help fulfil your goals and dreams, or it can drive you away from them. The way you focus affects your relationship with others.

> *Change your focus: Focus on the positive,*
> *and you'll start seeing others in a new light.*

**Change your focus:** Focus on the positive, and you'll start seeing others in a new light. In turn, this will influence the way you treat them and the way they treat you. Change starts on the inside. As Bakr bin Abdullah said, "If you see a man entrusted with other people's faults, forgetting his own, then know that he was deceived."

> *It is not the foolish who is a master of his people,*
> *but the one feigning foolishness.*

Instead of focusing on other people's wrongdoings and your differences, focus on your similarities, on things you agree on, and start strengthening them to reduce your differences. Rather than focusing on the dissimilarities between you and your boss, your husband, your friend, your son, appreciate their qualities; accept the universal truth that everyone is different. People can never have duplicate copies and no one will share all of your opinions, let alone be a copy of you! Al-Kindi (may he rest in peace) said, "He who only befriends the faultless will have few friends, he who only accepts his friends' loyalty will have much discontent, and he who reproaches his friends their every offence will have many enemies."

# Happy Thoughts

Studies have shown that focusing on differences reduces satisfaction and harmony in relationships by 70%. Your respect for other people's personalities makes you more capable of understanding and getting along with them

- You can't change others, but you can change the way you react to them. Focus on your similarities instead of your differences and appreciate their good qualities
- Most people can spot problems! This ability isn't a talent. But the person who can think up solutions instead of focusing on the problem can make a difference
- Dwelling on the past is destructive; it keeps you from enjoying your present and planning for your future. Whatever it was like, your past is over; you can't change it. Focus on today, so you have a better tomorrow
- Poverty is a state of mind. Everything we need to lead a prosperous life is always available and opportunities are limitless. If you focus on poverty, and the lack of opportunities and friends, that is what you'll get!
- Don't give too much thought to the people who hurt you and the things that annoy you. There are countless other thoughts that will benefit you, so focus on what makes you happy and ignore the trivialities

WHAT SHOULD I DO?
**Personal training:** Relationship management through focus.

**Do this exercise for 5 days:**
- ☛ Think of a loved one with whom you sometimes disagree
- ☛ Think of 3 qualities he has, such as being generous, fun, caring…
- ☛ Conjure up these qualities and keep them in mind
- ☛ Whenever you get into an argument with that person, before responding, think of these qualities
- ☛ You will notice that your anger has subsided and that you're more poised during the conversation
- ☛ You won't get results on the first try, but you certainly will through repetition

**Scientific study:**
"The Invisible Gorilla Experiment".

### What should I read?
*Notes from a Friend* by Anthony Robbins.

# PRESERVE YOUR STRENGTH

26. I Won't Give Up My Strength
27. The Results You Get = Circumstances + Your Response
28. Our Areas of Responsibility
29. It's My Father's Fault
30. Happy Thoughts

# I Won't Give Up My Strength

Your happiness is your responsibility. Try to live happily despite your circumstances; no one is guaranteed to satisfy and entertain you. Make the most out of life and live happily; happiness and unhappiness are a choice, and you are the one making it.

**That's what happened**
When employees of a certain company showed up to work one day, they were greeted by a big sign hanging on the front gate, which read, "The person who was hindering your progress, your happiness and your growth in this company died last night. We kindly ask you to enter and attend the funeral in the designated hall."

At first, all the employees were saddened by the death of their colleague, which some expected to be their manager and others, a co-worker who used to bother and hurt them. Then everyone became curious to know who that person standing between them and their progress and happiness was. They started going into the hall where the coffin was, with the company's security men making sure they were entering individually to see the person in the coffin. Surprisingly, each time someone would look inside the coffin, they would suddenly become speechless…as if something had touched their soul! In fact, lying at the bottom of the coffin was a mirror, reflecting the image of whoever was looking in. Next to it, a small sign read, "Only one person in this world can kill your ambition and your happiness: You."

Your life doesn't change along with your boss, friends, wife, company, place of work, or financial situation… You are the only person responsible for changing your life. It's very easy to give up our strength, our happiness and our goals, when we start blaming people and circumstances for our hardships. I can't exercise because there aren't any parks nearby and the weather is bad! I can't be at peace because of all the family drama. I can't be successful at work because my boss is too hard to please. I can't be happy, because of my looks and my tumultuous past. You may be right, but you can overcome these obstacles and lead a happy life, on one condition: to get rid of blame and excuses.

## Live According to the Principle that "No One Is Coming"

During a lecture at a university, Dr Branden, author of *The Six Pillars of Self-Esteem*, said to the students in attendance, "Live according to the principle that 'No one is coming'. No one is coming to take you to the island of happiness on a white horse; no one is coming to make your life better… You are responsible for your life, you are responsible for your self-esteem, you are responsible for your self-appreciation, you are responsible for your happiness, you are responsible for your self-development…"

Here, a student raised his hand and said, "Doctor, this statement is not true!"

So the doctor asked, "What do you mean by not true?"

The student answered, "You, Doctor, came to help us."

*You can rely on others in certain matters,*
*but there are things in life you must do on your own.*

So the doctor said, "Yes, I came, but only to tell you that 'no one is coming'. After this lecture, you are responsible for applying or ignoring what you learned."

You can rely on others in certain matters, but there are things in life you have to handle on your own, such as your health, your education, your job, your self-development, how you communicate with others…

Hence, the important rule for happiness and success is: "You have to take 100% responsibility for your own life." This means you have to stop blaming others, whining and complaining, looking for excuses, and waiting for the world to get better in order to be happy and at ease.

***As long as you blame people and circumstances, you are giving up your power and your happiness, and giving them the power to defeat you.***

I could be happy and have a better life if I weren't born in this city. If I had a better family, if I were richer, if my financial situation were better, if my friends were better, if I looked better, if my husband were different, if I could finish my education, if there were a gym nearby, if I were younger, if I were older…

If we surrender to such excuses, we become helpless, which will destroy our happiness and comfort. Indeed, the list of excuses is endless, and we always have a choice. We can either endure hardship and overcome our circumstances, or we can convince ourselves that these excuses are true and give in to them. But the result will be at the expense of our happiness and success… As long as you blame your relatives or your co-workers, your past or your genes, or traffic, or the weather, you are giving up your power and your happiness, and giving them the power to defeat you.

# The Results You Get = Circumstances + Your Response

Ahmad and Salman were born into a troubled family, with their father in jail for drug use, and their mother sick, unable to work. Ahmad was hard-working and responsible, while Salman neglected his studies and made bad friends. Even though both went to the same school and faced the same circumstances, Ahmad rejected these friends and ignored them, while Salman got along with them. At the end of high school, Ahmad graduated with honours and went on to study architecture in college, while Salman struggled and didn't finish his studies.

Ahmad applied himself in college. He studied hard for five years and once again graduated with honours. He got a prestigious job as an architect, with a salary of 15 thousand riyals; while Salman got a tough night job, only earning 4800 riyals.

Ahmad got married, had three children and bought his family a house. Meanwhile, Salman couldn't pay his rent on time, nor afford to buy his family a decent car.

Someone asked Ahmad what the secret to his success was. He answered, "My father's imprisonment and the circumstances we went through."

When Salman was asked what the reason behind his problems and struggles was, he answered, "My father's imprisonment and the circumstances we went through."

## THE RESULTS YOU GET = CIRCUMSTANCES + YOUR RESPONSE

Ahmad and Salman went through the same circumstances. But one had a victim's mentality, convincing himself that his life, his circumstances, his family, society as a whole, were responsible for his unhappiness and his failure; while the other thought differently. Ahmad decided that the choice was his, so he chose to live a happy life, rather than the one his father and the rest of his family lived. He also took full responsibility for his happiness, his life, his decisions and his choices.

The results you get = circumstances + your response.
R = c + r.

### *Two people can face the same circumstances, but get different results.*

Two people can face the same circumstances, but respond and react in different ways and get different results. One is like Ahmad, taking responsibility instead of giving in to his circumstances, so he becomes happier and more successful. Whereas the other struggles in life, because he keeps blaming his upbringing, his family… and believes that no matter what he does, he can't change the course of his life!

In truth, Salman is living the life he chose. It doesn't mean that he wished for his miserable situation, but that the life he currently leads is the result of his previous choices – or rather, not choosing to change his life. The same goes for anyone who chooses to think like a victim, blaming others and being passive in life. Naturally, he will get unpleasant results: weakness, unhappiness and a low standard of living. He will also feel like a victim does:

miserable, sad and defeated. This applies to all of us, as we are 100% responsible for everything that happens in our life. Every human being on this earth faces circumstances and challenges. Some think they are victims of these

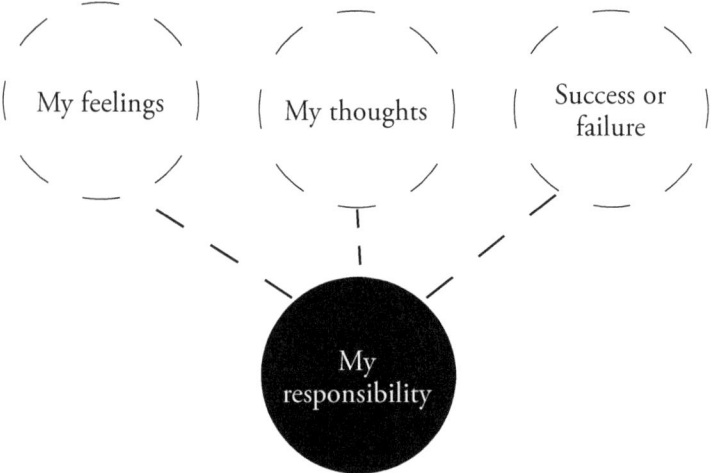

circumstances and are overcome with sadness and worry, living in defeat. Others take responsibility.

They think, "What can I do to improve my life?"

"I may not be able to control everything, but there is surely something I can do." Remember that, even in the toughest of circumstances, there's always something you can do.

Al-Bazzaz, a great scholar, told the incredible story of what he went through: "The Romans captured me while I was travelling and I remained in captivity for a year and a half. For five months, there were shackles around my neck and chains on my hands and feet, and my jailors would say to me, 'Say: Christ is the Son of God; we will do this and that to you.' But I always refused to. While in prison, there was a tutor who taught the boys Roman calligraphy, so I ended up learning the Byzantine script during captivity."

What if, God forbid, one of us was in his situation? He would think negative, discouraging thoughts, and fall prey to sorrow and distress. In contrast, someone who takes responsibility knows that there's always something he can do, even in the worst circumstances, like imprisonment. Indeed, he believes that a responsible person can't be stopped.

# Our Areas of Responsibility

1. You are responsible for your success and your failures. Two teenagers once saw a famous basketball player and one of them said, "He's so lucky, he was born talented!" The player overheard him, and told them, "You don't know how many hours I spend training every day." Whether it's training, a promotion, a certificate of excellence, or good relationships with the people you love; you are certainly responsible for it. You're the one who worked and – with God's blessing – put in the necessary effort to succeed.

This is the responsibility of success. It's very easy to acknowledge the role you play in your success but it's harder to take responsibility when things don't go your way: a failed relationship, a missed job opportunity, a financial loss…

Every day, the workers in a construction company would take their lunch break at 1 p.m. and eat the food they brought along. And every day, one of them would complain, "I don't like this meal. I'm sick of always eating bread and rice…"

One day, a friend of his said, "Buddy, we're sick of hearing you complain about your lunch every single day. If you don't like it, ask your wife to make you something else."

The grumpy worker said, "What wife are you talking about? I'm not married, I'm the one who made this meal!"

Isn't this the case for some people? They complain about

their circumstances, their friends, the tyranny of others, unemployment, having difficult studies… They can change all of this, or at the very least, improve their situation, but they don't! Here is the important question to ask: Will you take responsibility, or will you keep blaming circumstances, your environment, friends, the government, and so on?

2. You are responsible for your thoughts: At the start of a training session, the coach pointed to one student and said, "You're stupid!"

Then the coach asked the rest of the students, "Who thinks that my words will embarrass and upset this student?"

Most of them raised their hands. The coach said, "Those who answered 'Yes' are wrong, and those who answered 'No' are too!

It's not what I told this student that will raise or lower his self-confidence. Rather, it's what he will tell himself once I'm done talking. For example, if the student tells himself negative things, such as, 'The coach must have noticed something wrong with me. The other students will make fun of me, no doubt! Why do I always get myself into embarrassing situations…' Then the student's self-confidence will plummet, and he may stay silent from embarrassment, or have a fit of anger. He will be filled with negative feelings that upset him, and the reason is his thoughts.

However, if he tells himself, 'Poor coach, he doesn't even know me and he speaks ill of me! This coach has a no self-restraint.' Then his self-confidence will increase, and he will talk to me in a way that shows me he's in control of the situation. Thus, he will become happier and more confident."

This is why it's important for you to believe that

your thoughts – whether negative or positive – are your responsibility, and that you can control them.

3. You are responsible for your feelings. Some think that their feelings are caused by other people and outside circumstances. In reality, circumstances can affect us but we can either overcome them and rise above them or continue letting them be a source of unhappiness and misery. You can't live happily while blaming others. Circumstances can define you or they can inspire you. In addition to being a depressing mindset, blame requires energy and takes away your control over your own life because then, your happiness would depend on the words and actions of others, which is something you can't control!

***Some people might act in a way that bothers you, but you don't have to be angry or upset; you always have a choice.***

Remember that some people might act in a way that bothers you, but you don't have to be angry or upset. You always have a choice. You can ignore them, as you're not forced to listen to someone criticizing you; you can talk to them about their behaviour, and put a stop to it; or, if you have a duty towards them, you can consider it a test, and you will be rewarded for your patience.

Finally, remember that it's easy to make excuses for not achieving your goals, for living in misery, for finding your problems too hard to solve, or for your defeated mental state. Excuses are easy; we can make one for any situation. Traffic raises my blood pressure, my boss didn't give me an opportunity to shine, my dysfunctional family is the cause of my unhappiness…

One of the most important ways to be happy is to stop making excuses, blaming other people and circumstances, and complaining. This behaviour weakens you; it makes you give your power over to others and live as a victim, giving up your responsibility. You can always choose whether to be a product of your circumstances, or the one producing them. Indeed, negatively blaming others or looking for excuses make you a product of your circumstances, unlike positive self-blame – taking responsibility. For example, if a friend deceived you, negative blame would be to turn this deception into an obsession and lose your trust in everyone else; whereas positive blame is to learn not to trust blindly. And if you go out of business, negative blame is to hold the government or the economic situation responsible; whereas positive blame is knowing what you did wrong and learning from it, so you don't repeat it.

***Everything you go through will increase your merit and your reward.***

If, growing up, your family had a lot of problems, negative blame would be to lead an unhappy life. Whereas positive blame is to take responsibility, knowing that others had it worse than you and striving to fix what you can. It is to trust in God that everything you go through will increase your merit and your reward.

# It's My Father's Fault

Two brothers grew up in a troubled family. They had an alcoholic father who was wasteful of his family and a constant source of problems, in addition to never giving his sons the time of day. The brothers grew up to be very different people. One became a drug addict, neglectful of his family just like his father before him, even going to jail several times. As for the other, he turned his life around. He became a successful businessman, built a great, tight-knit family, and became a distinguished member of society. This intrigued one reporter, who decided to interview them to find out the secret behind their different fates – even though they lived the same circumstances, in the same house and with the same parents.

The son who wasted his life was asked, "You repeatedly went to prison, became addicted to drugs and lost your family; how did you get here?"

He answered, "What did you expect? I was born and grew up in a broken home, never getting any sense of stability. I would see my father abuse drugs and overly punish us, leading us astray. What did you expect? It's all my father's fault!"

The reporter asked the successful son the same question, "How did you get here? How did you achieve this success, building a fortune and a great family?"

He answered, "What did you expect? I was born and grew up in a broken home, never getting any sense of stability.

I would see my father abuse drugs and overly punish us, leading us astray. What did you expect? I learnt from my father, so that I wouldn't lead a life as miserable as his!"

Don't doubt for a single moment that we are the reason behind our problems or our happiness. No matter the circumstances, our choices will always be a major reason for what we get out of life. "It is for what your hands have earned."

Happiness or misery, success or failure: the choice is in your hands. So is the absence of choice, which would leave you at the mercy of circumstances. That would also be a choice, though a bad one.

> *When you take responsibility and stop blaming everything and everyone else, you will become more powerful and in control of your life.*

Whether you want to or not, the person you see when you look in the mirror is a mixture of your problems and their solution. When you take responsibility and stop blaming everything and everyone else, you will become more powerful and in control of your life.

# Happy Thoughts

I am happy to take responsibility for my success, my failure, my thoughts and my feelings: I am never giving up my power

- ➤ I am improving myself now, to become who I'm meant to be
- ➤ I accept responsibility for my feelings. From now on, no one can upset me or make me feel inferior without my consent
- ➤ I might not be able to change my circumstances but I always have the choice to do something about them, no matter how small
- ➤ I am responsible for my quality of life and I will take the initiative to change anything that isn't fulfilling me
- ➤ I am now changing my life for the better. I won't wait for people to change in order for my life to improve. As of now, I will stop blaming others
- ➤ I am responsible for the future I want

## What should I do?
During Responsibility Week, you should get rid of:

| | |
|---|---|
| Excuses | When you want to do something important to you or get rid of a bad habit, your mind will always conjure up excuses to back down and give up. This week, don't let any excuse defeat you. |
| Blame | When you're in distress: don't blame anyone; it would only add to your weakness and misery. Ignore any thoughts of blaming others, pray for yourself and your loved ones, and think of positive actions that will bring you closer to your goals. |
| Complaining | Excessive complaining to other people makes you vulnerable and increases your negativity towards yourself and others. Each time you notice yourself complaining, stop and replace the complaint with positive words. |

## What should I read?
*The Patience of The Pious Predecessors in Seeking Knowledge* by Abdul Fattah Abu Guddah.
*Notes from a Friend* by Anthony Robbins.

# POSITIVE FEELINGS ARE THE PATH TO HAPPINESS

31. What Are You Nourishing?
32. Positive Feelings
33. Positive Feelings Broaden Your Horizons
34. Eliminate 100% of Your Negative Feelings
35. Your Positivity Ratio

# What Are You Nourishing?

When you focus on things you can't change, you drown in anger and grief. Instead, accept what you can't change and focus on what you can. You will become more positive.

**That's what happened**
There once was a man from Alaska who owned two huge tigers. He would hold weekly events that centred around the two animals fighting. And every week, crowds would flock from the village to partake in this event and bet on the tiger fight. Naturally, when a tiger wins, so do those who bet on him; so the enthusiasm was high. The results were unpredictable. Some weeks one tiger would win and other weeks the other would be victorious, making it difficult to predict the winner. Still, a villager was surprised to notice that the owner of the tigers always made a winning bet, which meant that he knew the result beforehand.

The villager went to see the owner, and asked him how he could tell which tiger would win.

The owner said to him, "Well, I will tell you, but only if you promise to keep it a secret."

The villager promised, after which the owner said, "It's very easy to tell! The tiger I nourish all week is the one who wins and the tiger I starve all week is the one who loses!"

This is one secret to happiness. Ask yourself: which

feelings are you nourishing?

A lot of people don't know why they're unhappy, unable to enjoy life. Simply put, the reason is that they trained their mind in negative feelings: worry, complaining, whining, hatred, despair and negative focus. When you nourish positive feelings such as joy, gratitude, wonder, love, hope and positive curiosity, you multiply your happiness, your well-being and your mental health, in addition to expanding your horizons, your ability to make the right choices and your communication skills.

# Positive Feelings

Joy, pleasure and optimism aren't the only positive feelings; there's a wide variety of them. The more we live these feelings at the right time and nourish them, the more they contribute to our success and happiness, in addition to strengthening our personality. Conversely, negative feelings limit our thinking and make us reclusive and emotionally rigid, effectively turning us into an inflexible person in whom nothing moves, who doesn't care what happens to him. Some of the main positive feelings are:

➤ **Happiness/Joy:** when something good happens to you or when your wish comes true, feeling cheerful indicates that you're happy. It also nourishes your positive feelings, strengthens your personality and even becomes an asset in negative situations. The feeling of joy is accompanied by a desire to communicate with others and share your happiness with them. Hence, joy doesn't just make you happy, it improves your relationships, too.

*When we overlook God's blessings and focus on the negative aspects of our life, or on what we don't want, we sacrifice our happiness.*

➤ **Gratitude/appreciating our blessings:** one of the positive feelings that contribute the most to our happiness is being aware of our blessings. Indeed, the seeds of sorrow and misery can't grow in a thankful heart. When we ignore and overlook God's blessings and focus on the negative aspects of our life, or on what we don't want, we sacrifice our happiness. If you're not happy today, or you're depressed, the fastest way to get over this state is to stop focusing on what you don't have, counting your blessings instead, and thanking God for them. Remember that giving thanks for your blessings benefits you first. Your happiness, comfort, health and success all depend on acknowledging your blessings and giving thanks for them. As God in His wisdom says: "And whoever is grateful – his gratitude is only for [the benefit of] himself."

*Learn about your own moments of peace. Some find it in reverence, some in relaxation and others in a restful vacation.*

➤ **Peace and mental clarity:** throughout their life, everyone has moments of mental clarity. These moments consist of feeling safe, peaceful, free from troubles, problems, worries and other polluting thoughts. Clarity gives you strength and energy. More importantly, it's part of what generates happiness, since you can't spend your life riddled with thoughts and worries; the flood of thoughts would break you. So your capacity for clarity and peace is an energy that pushes you forward. Learn about your own moments of peace. Some find it in reverence, some in relaxation, others in a restful vacation, in moments of solitude, or a quick nap.

- **Passion:** passion is a positive curiosity that spreads in its owner, providing him with the determination to know everything going on around him and the drive to improve. Passion keeps you in a state of inspiration and anticipation. Feelings of passion are inspiring and joyful; they are the driving force behind your life and your thoughts. They turn you into an aspiring person who accomplishes their goals. As James Baldwin wrote, "Fires can't be made with dead embers, nor can enthusiasm be stirred by spiritless men."
- **Hope:** hope gives you motivation in work and in life, while also improving your relationships. Without hope, there are no accomplishments, no appetite for life. Rather, the future becomes grim in the eyes of its owner. Consequently, he won't recover from an illness, improve a relationship, or succeed in a project… nothing will go right. This is a pessimistic outlook that ruins his life, so that even if he owns the world and everything in it, he will know no peace. That is because he expects and waits for the worst, and questions God's will! Hope, or optimism, is one of the secrets to happiness, success, health and good relationships. When you're armed with it, if your life is going well, you always expect better, and if something is worrying you, you expect that it will get better.
- **Inspiration:** inspiration is an important positive feeling that drives you to learn from people or circumstances and pushes you to strive for excellence. It also breaks the barrier of rigidity and despair that sometimes seep into the soul. Inspiration is a positive feeling that increases our happiness levels. Do you

have any heroes? Make a list of them, study their life and the hardships they faced. It's one way of sparking up inspiration. Other ways include curiosity, a love of learning, pushing your limits and taking calculated risks. Even your problems can be an inspiration!

➤ **Wonder:** wonder is the spontaneous positive feeling we get when we encounter something awe-inspiring – whether in nature or in something man-made, in other people or in ourselves. Not only does the feeling of wonder make you happy and improve your health (as you will read in the chapter dedicated to the subject); it also increases your qualities and your merit. When you see something wonderous, don't just stand there stiffly, but rather, praise the God and say, "Glory to God."

➤ **Love:** love is the highest kind of positive feelings, rather it's what brings all these feelings together. Without love, you wouldn't appreciate your blessings nor be optimistic about a good relationship; nothing will inspire you and you won't be passionate about anything. For you could never plant any seeds in a barren land. Love can transcend humans and living beings to inanimate things: a land, a job, a car. Sometimes, you even find yourself loving something because someone you love loves it. Hence, love can be a positive contagion. Love spreads happiness in your life; because love is patient, love is kind. It does not envy, it does not boast, it is not proud. It does not dishonour others, it is not self-seeking, it is not easily angered, it keeps no record of wrongs. It is joyous, and brings joy. It trusts, and protects, and endures.

# Positive Feelings Broaden Your Horizons

A researcher did an experiment with two groups of students. With the first group, he discussed negative events and situations that happened to them in the past and talked about the future in a pessimistic way. As for the second, he talked to them in a positive, optimistic way and reminded them of their strengths. At the end of each conversation, the researcher asked the group about their future prospects and plans.

The answers of the negative group were limited, their choices focused on steering clear of problems, poverty and unemployment. In contrast, the second group came up with diverse and original ideas, and had a broader perspective than the first group.

***Positive emotions such as joy, contentment and passion can increase your awareness and expand your mind.***

This is a popular scientific theory, called the 'Broaden-and-Build' theory. It states that positive feelings such as joy, contentment and passion can increase your awareness and expand your mind, making you wiser and more creative. They can also make you more open to the many choices you have, unlike negative feelings, which narrow your perspective and make you short-sighted in your decisions. Indeed, a scared or worried individual usually only has two choices: either run away from what's scaring him or face it! He's like someone who encounters a predator who has only two choices: fight or flight. Positive feelings, however, give us a lot of choices. For instance, when you're passionate about something, you start looking forward to the future... I want to learn more, I want to know the next steps, I want a better future, I want further reading and knowledge... When we feel at ease, our minds open up, and we strive to better ourselves. Think about yourself in happy times... Don't you want to play and have fun, to do many things, and give, and communicate positively with others? When we're feeling glad, we interact positively with those around us, with more wisdom and poise.

***Contentment isn't lack of ambition. I can be content while still remaining ambitious, and striving for more.***

Similarly, the feeling of contentment allows us to live in the moment, appreciating what we have, the circumstances we're going through and the relationships we're surrounded with. It also makes us wiser in dealing with circumstances we don't like, because they stop being in total control of our thoughts. Moreover, contentment isn't lack of ambition. I can be content while still remaining ambitious and striving for more. Contentment is appreciating and being satisfied with what you have, while being ambitious and planning for a better future.

As for the feelings of love and affection in our relationships, they are an integral part of our happiness. Humans are intrinsically social creatures who need to feel

## POSITIVE FEELINGS BROADEN YOUR HORIZONS

love, belonging and appreciation from those around them. The solitary person always suffers from anxiety, boredom, loneliness, nervousness and low self-esteem. That is why love provides humans with happiness, tranquillity, safety and mental comfort, thus producing a healthy, psychologically balanced personality. When you love your work you excel at it, adding your own touch and always looking to improve it. And when you love your friends, your neighbours or your relatives, you build bridges between you, overlook their mistakes and build broader relationships… Love, like other positive feelings, broadens your horizons, elevates you and makes your life soar.

The choice is in your hands. You can nourish negative feelings or positive ones. Positive feelings will open up the road for you and broaden your horizons, turning you into a positive person. Whereas negative feelings will bring you down, limit your choices and reduce you to a fight-or-flight mindset! Watch what you think about, what you say and who you befriend. Be aware of daily situations and your reactions to them. Take a moment of awareness, and be mindful of your feelings: how many times a day do you feel angry, indignant, worried, afraid? How many times do you feel satisfied, joyful, passionate, loved? Every time you feel something, you nourish it, making it stronger and its effect on your life bigger. And when you make its effect bigger, it controls your perspective on life, your decisions, your actions, and all areas of your life.

***Starving your feelings is to limit nourishing them, communicating with them and continuously living them.***

Hence, it's important for you to know that starving your feelings – whether negative or positive – is to limit nourishing them, communicating with them and continuously living them. Make sure you starve your negative feelings and nourish the positive ones. For example, if you let a happy moment pass you by without experiencing it, you are starving your positive feelings. And if you let any little thing upset you, or if you overly complain, watch sad news and befriend negative people, don't be surprised when your anger, tension, worry, fear… when your misery increases, and your happiness decreases. Because then you would be nourishing negative feelings and strengthening the black tiger inside you!

On a given day, think of a positive feeling you want to nourish, like love, gratitude, contentment, passion, joy… Then, focus on talking and reading about it, as well as befriending people and doing things that make you feel it… Thus, you would be nourishing positive feelings and strengthening the white tiger inside you. And that tiger will win your inner war.

# Eliminate 100% of Your Negative Feelings

We may hear in some courses or lectures, or read in some articles the catch phrase, "Eliminate 100% of your negative feelings." Such promises may seem tempting and attractive, but are they useful to you, and do they make sense?! It's impossible to avoid all negative feelings because living means facing obstacles and struggles. Good and bad things as well as troubles happen to all of us, and if anyone was going to be spared, it would have been the Prophet (peace be upon him).

***All feelings, whether negative or positive, are important and serve a goal. We can't completely eliminate our negative feelings.***

All feelings, whether negative or positive, are important and serve a particular goal in each person's life. We can't eliminate our negative feelings. For instance, if you face a sudden, imminent danger, like a speeding car or a predator, fear would be positive in this case because it saves your life. You can't just stop and think positively or look for happiness in the face of such imminent danger!

Similarly, when you lose someone dear, or part with a friend or loved one, sadness here helps wash away the pain, since you're a human being, not an emotionless robot. Additionally, sadness decreases the risk of depression and signals to others that we need help.

Guilt and regret are also important. When you make a mistake, or fail at something, these feelings are a reminder to not repeat that mistake! They help you learn from your past experiences, deter you from tyranny and injustice, and make you act morally when you wrong others.

In fact, stress, sadness, and other negative feelings are an important part of life. Recent research suggests that experiencing and accepting these feelings is essential to our mental health. Indeed, suppressing them can be counterproductive, to the point that it can diminish our sense of satisfaction!

## *Excessive suffering over someone doesn't prove that you love them.*

Negative feelings become a problem when they control your life, or when they're uncalled for. Our Prophet was grieved when his son Ibrahim passed away, but his grief lasted for a limited time, which isn't a sign of hardheartedness – God forbid. Excessive sadness over someone doesn't benefit them. It mainly harms you, impeding your happiness and peace of mind. Excessive suffering over someone doesn't prove that you love them. It just means that you would rather entertain negative thoughts and feelings that are meant to isolate you from everything beautiful. Excessive suffering only proves that you're self-destructive.

We now know that all feelings are useful and positive when you need them and when it's the right time for them. But even positive feelings become "negative" if their timing is wrong.

For example, when someone close to you loses a loved one, being happy at their funeral would be inappropriate, because you need sadness and sorrow to sympathize with the bereaved. Feeling sadness and pain can be positive at such a time.

All feelings, whether positive or negative, help us cope with the situation at hand. The key is to find the right balance between the two!

# Your Positivity Ratio

How many positive feelings do we need? What is the right happiness level? Those are important questions to address. In one study on happy marriages and relationships, it was found that a happy marriage has a positivity ratio of at least 3:1, meaning three positive things for every negative one. If the ratio is 2:1 or less, it means that the relationship is bad.

Thus, the "positivity ratio" saw the light. It's an easy way to measure your happiness that makes you aware and conscious of it. You can find out what your ratio is through knowing the effect that events and situations have on your feelings. Since this test indicates your positivity ratio on the previous day, you can do it once a week for a month, at the end of which you will get a clear idea about your happiness level.

To do this test, think of the previous day. Think about the events and situations you experienced and how you communicated with yourself and others, then answer the questions below. Then, calculate your positivity ratio and see how happy you are compared to the norm.

## YOUR POSITIVITY RATIO

| 1 | Did you find something fun or entertaining? | o Not at all  o A little  o Average  o Above average  o A lot |
|---|---|---|
| 2 | Did you hear or see something that amazed you? | o Not at all  o A little  o Average  o Above average  o A lot |
| 3 | Did you feel satisfied with your life? | o Not at all  o A little  o Average  o Above average  o A lot |
| 4 | Did you feel grateful for something? | o Not at all  o A little  o Average  o Above average  o A lot |
| 5 | Did you feel optimistic? | o Not at all  o A little  o Average  o Above average  o A lot |
| 6 | Did you feel motivated or encouraged? | o Not at all  o A little  o Average  o Above average  o A lot |
| 7 | Did you feel positive curiosity/passion? | o Not at all  o A little  o Average  o Above average  o A lot |
| 8 | Did you feel happy and cheerful? | o Not at all  o A little  o Average  o Above average  o A lot |
| 9 | Did you feel love or closeness? | o Not at all  o A little  o Average  o Above average  o A lot |
| 10 | Did you feel trustful? | o Not at all  o A little  o Average  o Above average  o A lot |

| 11 | Did you feel distrustful? | o Not at all  o A little  o Average  o Above average  o A lot |
| --- | --- | --- |
| 12 | Did you feel angry or upset? | o Not at all  o A little  o Average  o Above average  o A lot |
| 13 | Did you feel ashamed or insulted? | o Not at all  o A little  o Average  o Above average  o A lot |
| 14 | Did you feel repulsed or disgusted? | o Not at all  o A little  o Average  o Above average  o A lot |
| 15 | Did you feel embarrassed? | o Not at all  o A little  o Average  o Above average  o A lot |
| 16 | Did you feel like blaming yourself? | o Not at all  o A little  o Average  o Above average  o A lot |
| 17 | Did you feel hatred? | o Not at all  o A little  o Average  o Above average  o A lot |
| 18 | Did you feel sad? | o Not at all  o A little  o Average  o Above average  o A lot |
| 19 | Did you feel afraid? | o Not at all  o A little  o Average  o Above average  o A lot |
| 20 | Did you feel nervous? | o Not at all  o A little  o Average  o Above average  o A lot |

## Instructions for finding out and evaluating your score:

- Grade your answers as follows: Not at all: 0; A little: 1; Average: 2; Above average: 3; A lot: 4.
- Tally up the results for questions 1 to 10.
- Tally up the results for questions 11 to 20.
- Divide the result of questions 1 to 10 by the result of questions 11 to 20. For example, if you scored 30 on questions 1 to 10 and 10 on questions 11 to 20, your positivity ratio would be: My positivity ratio = 30 ÷ 10 = 3/1, which means 3 positive feelings for every negative feeling.

## Score evaluation

1/1 means that you lead an unhappy life and need to put in more effort and work to improve your happiness level.

2/1 means that your life is leaning towards happiness. But there are obstacles to this happiness, just as there are areas where it hasn't been achieved, so it's important to strive to achieve it in order to reach better happiness levels.

3/1 means that you are leading a happy life, with room to further increase your happiness.

4/1 is the highest happiness level.

Note that, as we already mentioned, negative feelings can't be completely absent. Life can't be devoid of them, but what's important is developing positive feelings.

### What should I do?

**Positivity Week:** Here are some ideas to infuse your week with happiness:

- Pay attention to your thoughts and words, always choosing positive thoughts

- Mind what you watch. Watch fewer negative news programmes and series that focus on problems, causing depression and sadness. Watch things that calm you down instead
- Love yourself and those around you. Always let yourself feel your love for your family, relatives, friends and even strangers
- Don't let happy moments pass you by. Savour even the happiness that the little things give you. Feel happy waking up, watching the sun rise, or a seeing stranger smile
- Strive to learn and better yourself: passion broadens your horizons. Opt for a book or an educational or cultural program that expands your knowledge and your mind
- Every day, stop, even for five minutes, and contemplate the blessings God bestowed upon you, your family and people around you. Meditate on these blessings until relief washes over you
- Keep the morning and evening Remembrances in mind and reflect on the thanks, gratitude and sense of blessings that they contain

## What should I read?
*You Can Heal Your Life*, by Louise Hay.

# LIVE YOUR FEELINGS, BE HAPPY

36. Appreciate the Little Pleasures
37. Don't Wait for a Miracle to Be Happy
38. Create Your Own Opportunities for Happiness

# Appreciate the Little Pleasures

Don't postpone any happy moment that comes your way. Live each moment, as you may not get a repeat. Rejoice at every little thing you experience, no matter how simple that joy is…

**That's what happened**
A poor man passed away after a lifelong struggle with poverty. He was known in his surroundings to be needy and miserable. After his death, his family went to his tiny apartment to clear it out and sell, or rather throw away, his worthless belongings.

While they were walking around the apartment, a number of wall paintings caught the attention of one of his relatives – an art expert. He believed they were unusual and valuable. So the family decided to have them evaluated by a specialist. And big surprise: these paintings, done by famous artists, were expensive, and could make them all rich!

The poor man who owned these paintings wasn't able to appreciate them, because he didn't know their value, so he lived a life of misery and deprivation.

This is the case for many people: they have many reasons to be happy, but they're very easily blinded by their troubles, problems and responsibilities, to the point where they forget the happy moments and despair. They have problems at work, bills to pay, children to raise, difficult people to deal with. Gradually, they begin to lose their smile, becoming serious and formal, rarely laughing.

***Enjoying life gives you strength when times are hard and helps you overcome its problems and challenges.***

Even when you have responsibilities, you can still be cheerful. You can work hard at your job and still enjoy life. Enjoying life gives you strength when times are hard and helps you overcome its problems and challenges.

Our Prophet (peace be upon him) had the most and the hardest responsibilities. Still, one of his companions said, "I have not seen anyone who smiled more than the Prophet." He also often joked with people of all ages and even once raced his wife!

There was a man from the people of the desert whose name was Zahir bin Haram. He would always give the Prophet (peace be upon him) gifts and he was loved by the Prophet (peace be upon him). He was also not of a pleasant facial appearance. The Prophet (peace be upon him) came to him one day, while he was selling his goods, and embraced him from behind so that Zahir could not see who it was. Zahir exclaimed, "Let me go, who is this?" Then he turned and found it was the Prophet (peace be upon him), so he continued to cling onto his chest. Upon this, the Prophet (peace be upon him) said in jest to those around him, "Who would like to buy a slave?" So Zahir said, "O Prophet, by God you will find me to be of no value." The Prophet (peace be upon him) answered, "But to God you are valuable."

# Don't Wait for a Miracle to Be Happy

Bronnie Ware, a nurse, was at the deathbed of many elderly patients. She would always ask them, "What are your biggest regrets in life?" They all had one answer in common: "We let the happy moments pass us by, but experienced the sad ones fully. We didn't realize that happiness is a personal choice until it was too late. We had forgotten this in the midst of our daily life struggles."

There's a saying that "Only the cheerful see the beauty of life," and that is what makes them the happiest of people.

Life is short; too short to be wasted on anger, complaints and misery. Therefore, it is important to make the best of it, to live and enjoy every moment, look for opportunities for happiness and experience this feeling in your daily life.

*Smile at least once a day and remember that laughter is a natural stress reliever.*

The world is a fun place, so allow yourself to be happy, to laugh. Watch entertaining programmes, laugh with your family and friends, watch entertaining shows in your city, read upbeat novels and stories. Laugh with the salesman, or any person you meet for the first time. Everyone has their own way of being happy and their own sense of humour, but it's important to make happiness a part of your life and the life of those around you. Make sure to smile at least once a day and remember that laughter is a natural stress reliever.

Some people wait for a special occasion to be joyous and have fun, such as going on holiday, getting a reward, starting a new relationship, better health. And it's true, these things can bring us happiness.

But why should we wait for these things to happen? Why should we wait for the right reason and the right time to be happy?

If we think this way, we miss out on real happinesses, which are the little moments of happiness in our daily life. Indeed, every day can be a happy one when we just breathe and feel that we're living in a beautiful world. This is the right way of thinking and it raises your happiness level. Don't postpone your happiness until big things happen.

Beware of the trap of delaying happiness and remember that you can be happy while on the road to success. At one stage or another in their life, most people feel that they shouldn't be happy unless they reach a certain goal. You find yourself saying, "I will be happy when:

I graduate college.

I get a job.

I get married.

I lose weight."

And the list goes on; it's endless! Before you know it, your life has passed you by, and you didn't let any happiness in!

# Create Your Own Happy Occasions

Don't wait for the weekend, a long vacation or a special occasion to be happy and cheerful. Rejoice in the simple, everyday things: returning home, meeting loved ones, learning something new, watching an entertaining program, getting a nice letter, going out, getting dressed, paying your bills, praying with the Congregation, ending your fast. Every act, however small, can brighten up your day. Your days may not all be happy, but there are bound to be good things in every one of them, for God's blessings upon us are countless.

*Those who laugh together, stay together. No one wants to befriend miserable people.*

Sometimes, there is a pressing need for us to set aside our tasks and indulge in life's small pleasures, which doesn't require a lot of time and effort. Ask yourself, when was the last time you went on a walk and enjoyed the breeze? When did you enjoy your favourite game with a loved one? Such simple occasions cure you and heal your heart. Remember that the best things in life are simple!

These joyful daily moments energise you, nurture your happiness and make your relationships with others friendlier and more enjoyable. A family that has fun together stays strong, and friends who laugh together, stay together… No one wants to befriend miserable people.

CREATE YOUR OWN HAPPY OCCASIONS

A happy person is cheerful at the start of his day; he wakes up happy, knowing that it's a blessing. He thanks God for reviving him after a night of slumber, rejoices at the sight of his family, the smile of someone dear. He's happy going to school or work, meeting his friends, watching the rain fall.

You don't need to have a lot of money to be happy. Look for happiness in the small pleasures of everyday life and indulge in them. Never let them pass you by with the excuse that you're busy! As long as you're alive, work will never end.

A friend once told me a story about him and his father. He recounted: "I was giving dad a ride to our village. I was speeding, because I had software to install back home, so he asked me to slow down. I told him I was busy. Coincidentally, we were passing by a cemetery, so he answered, 'Son, all the people in this cemetery left this world with unfinished business! Let's enjoy the ride, and you'll get back to your things soon enough'."

Sometimes, we drown in the hustle and bustle of life, thus forgetting ourselves, those around us and our happiness. Make time for your family and friends and, most importantly, for yourself. Make yourself, and those around you happy and glad. Happiness prolongs life, improves health and increases creativity. If you made yourself and your family happy, you would be doing them a favour and doing them good. Dutifulness is not only to listen and obey: it's also to benefit those to whom you are dutiful.

***Make enjoying the small pleasures of life your priority, as they nurture and increase your happiness.***

Make enjoying the little pleasures of life your priority, as these pleasures – such as a family gathering, someone's success, someone else's recovery, a loved one's homecoming, enjoying nature, an evening with friends, accomplishing something at work or at home and many more – nurture and increase your happiness. When you make yourself and others happy, you will attract happiness and happy people. As the saying goes, "Keep a green tree in your heart and the singing bird will come." Hence, for you to be happy, it's very important to let yourself feel that happiness and spread it in your life as well as the life of those around you. Don't let happy moments pass you by, but rather, celebrate the simplest achievement. Indeed, some of us can't be happy with their accomplishments, even though our days are filled with them… Your fast is an achievement, as is your smile, and your dutifulness. Remember that your cheerfulness multiplies your happiness, makes your life well-balanced and relieves its stress and troubles.

#### What should I do?
Live your feelings. Live the feeling of joy throughout your day.

Rejoice in meeting your family or friends and cheer them up; play with a child; go to a nearby park; enjoy a meal you love; enjoy drinking coffee or tea and sharing this pleasure with others; walk barefoot in the sand and feel its grains under your feet; smell the rain; be happy accomplishing a daily task at home or at work; forgive someone who wronged you, conjure up happiness for yourself and for him; go through old photo albums; watch your favourite show; watch a sunset or sunrise; read your favourite book in a quiet spot; go to a coffee shop or a nearby garden… Rejoice in things that didn't use to cross your mind.

#### What should I read?
*Live Life Like Never Before*, by Shukla Datta.

# LIVE YOUR FEELINGS, BE THANKFUL

39. Count Your Blessings
40. Gratitude Is the Way to Happiness
41. Appreciate Your Blessings
42. Bad Habits

# Count Your Blessings

Thanksgiving brings happiness. Thank God for everything. If you witness a beautiful sunrise, give thanks; if you sit with loved ones, give thanks. Give thanks for everything, no matter how small, because gratitude gives you a dose of happiness.

**That's what happened**
A man woke up one day with backache but he was too busy with his daily tasks to pay attention to the pain. He dropped his children off at school in his usual bad mood,

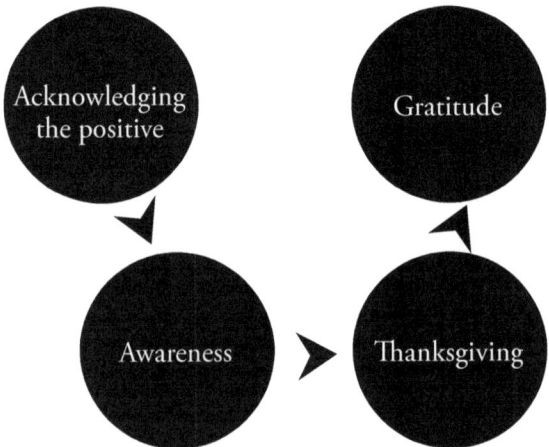

inevitably shouting at someone for no good reason.

He went to work fuming from bad traffic, wishing he

could have stayed at home; but he had to work. As the days went by his pain increased at work and he felt that he needed painkillers.

Indeed, when he took painkillers, his pain subsided temporarily. But at midnight, it came back worse – so strong that he screamed in agony. Barely able to move, he managed go to casualty. Once initial test results were produced, the doctor came to him with painful news: "We suspect that you have a life-threatening tumour and you need an urgent operation before it spreads. There is a big chance that the spinal cord will be affected and you won't be able to walk again!"

The man was in shock. He was confused, unable to process what he had heard. A hundred thoughts were going through his head. Who will take care of my children? How will I live? How will I go to work? How, how, how… an endless list of painful questions.

After his surgery, he awoke with a blurry vision, barely able to move his lips. A few minutes later, upon entering his room and seeing him, his wife and children started to cry, and he joined them. Then the doctor came in, this time with good news: "The operation was a success and you will be able to walk again, God willing!"

Do we really need to lose our blessings to realise their worth? At that moment, the man said, "Praise be to God for a clear eye, a healthy body, a beating heart and a good family. Praise be to you, God, for your countless blessings."

# Gratitude Is the Way to Happiness

A lot of people don't know why they're unhappy, unable to enjoy their life. One of the main reasons for unhappiness is training the mind to worry, to complain and to focus on the negative. That is why you can never be happy and ungrateful at the same time – even if you were the richest, prettiest, smartest, healthiest person on earth! One of the most important habits that increase happiness and make us think positively is being aware of our blessings and thankful for them; or what is known as 'gratitude'.

Gratitude starts with acknowledging the positive things in your life, being aware of them, then thanking God for them and for his countless other blessings. Gratitude is giving thanks to God, other people, anything and everything that has an influence over your life, your happiness and your peace of mind. Someone who doesn't give thanks to other people, is being ungrateful to God. And if he's ungrateful to God, he will live in misery, unable to appreciate anything good in his life. Gratitude is a secret to happiness, success and achieving your goals. It's a source of abundance and blessings, because a grateful heart is a magnet that attracts good things to your life. Gratitude is the greatest act of worship. The first line in Surah Al-Fatihah (The chapter 'The Opening') is Al-Hamd (The Praise), which is a show of gratitude to God. Therefore,

Satan strives to make you unthankful and to divert you from gratitude by any means: "There will I come upon them from their front and from their backs and from their right and from their left so that You will not find most of them grateful (to You)."

Gratitude is a telescope that makes you see and realise the blessings around you.

***The more grateful you are, the better your financial situation, your mental state, your relationships and everything else will be.***

If we look around, we will all find plenty of blessings everywhere around us. All you need is to stop a little, open your eyes, acknowledge your blessings and thank God for them. Don't let them pass you by or ignore them. Rather, stand in awe of them, like someone looking at something for the first time. The more you contemplate, think and acknowledge these blessings, the bigger their positive impact on your happiness and your life will be.

And the more grateful you are, the better your life will be. Furthermore, this improvement doesn't only concern material things. It also extends to other areas like relationships, places, beautiful experiences, circumstances and opportunities. In fact, a lot of studies prove the importance of gratitude for relationships, happiness, success. One study reported by the Psychological Society even concluded that "increased gratitude reflects positively on people's lives in terms of satisfaction, happiness, positivity, and hope."

# Appreciate Your Blessings

The quickest way to rid yourself of distress is to stop focusing on what you don't have. Focus on what you have instead and thank God for it. Look for reasons to be thankful; gratitude can solve all your problems.

You might think this statement is exaggerated and say, "Let's be realistic, the traffic on my way to work is unbearable and the weather is scorching hot, so you can't blame me for complaining!" Still, I say to you: be thankful for what you have. There are people who wish to own your car, to be in your place and go to your job every day.

*If you can walk, and talk, and think, and see, you already have something that money can't buy.*

You may think, "If I had enough money, I would be grateful, happy and optimistic!" Then I would tell you: change your perspective! You may not have as much money as you wish for, but you have your health, which is a priceless gift. Indeed, many people who have millions suffer from illnesses that money can't cure and would give their fortune in exchange for good health. If you can walk, and talk, and think, and see, you already have something that money can't buy. Someone once confided, "I used to complain about not owning a good pair of shoes, until I met someone who had lost his legs. I realised then how lucky I am!"

## APPRECIATE YOUR BLESSINGS

If you have food in your fridge, clothes on your back and a roof over your head, you are among the 75% richest people on earth.

If you have a small bank account and some bills in your wallet, then you are among the 80% richest people on earth.

If you woke up this morning in one piece, with just a few minor health problems, you are in a better condition than a million people around the world who won't make it to the end of the week.

If you have never experienced the dangers and tragedies of war, you have it better than 20 million people who suffer from war and homelessness.

If you were never subjected to any torture in prison or detention and your family didn't suffer from famine, then you're doing better than 500 million people around the world who still suffer from such plights!

***In every situation and in every circumstance, we can find a reason to be thankful, and gratitude is the secret to a happy life.***

When you see a homeless person, pray for him, thank God for giving you a home and help him if you can.

When you see a handicapped person in a wheelchair, pray for him and thank God for the gift of walking.

If you can't sleep and start feeling anxious, think of those who don't have a bed nor a shelter.

If you drive through a difficult, busy or bumpy road, instead of becoming angry, think of those who don't own a car.

When you face problems at work, instead of letting it ruin your life, think of those who don't have any job at all!

Instead of wishing for a better wife and complaining about the one you have, try to think of your wife's wonderful qualities. Then, she will become more loving towards you and you will be more appreciative of her.

Instead of complaining about your salary and your boss, thank God for having a job. Then, you will perform better, become more creative and increase your chances of a promotion.

In every situation and in every circumstance, we can find a reason to be thankful, and gratitude is the secret to a happy life. Hence, always remember how blessed you are and thank God for that.

When you stop complaining and being indignant and start focusing on your blessings, you will get more of what you want. It's a fact of life: "If you give thanks, I will give you more."

**Live Your Feelings**
Live the feelings of gratitude throughout your day.

Thank God in front of your children for the tiniest of blessings; thank God when you solve a problem or accomplish something; thank God when you eat or drink, when you're happy and when you're sitting with loved ones… Thank your wife in front of your children, thank your children, thank everyone who is good to you, thank your friends. Thank the janitor; thank the one who let you pass him in line, or let you go first, or gave you directions; surprise your boss by thanking him…

Live feelings of gratitude so that they reflect on your happiness and multiply your success. Turn these feelings into action: "Work, O House of David, and give thanks."

# Bad Habits

A villager who was married with kids wasn't pleased with his life. He visited a sage to complain about his small home, his grumpy wife and his irritating children. The wise man said he would help him, but only if he followed his instructions, and the villager agreed.

The sage asked, "Are there any hens in your barn?" The villager answered, "Yes."

The sage ordered, "Bring them inside for the week." The villager said, "But the house is tiny!"

The sage repeated, "Bring the hens inside for the week."

The villager complied. A week later, he went to the wise man, complaining, "They're noisy, dirty, their feathers are everywhere… O wise man, our house has become more miserable, and my wife and children more annoying."

The sage asked, "Do you have a sheep in your barn?" The villager answered, "Yes."

The sage said, "Bring it inside for the week as well."

Shocked, the villager exclaimed, "No way, wise man!"

The sage said, "Do as you're told, like we agreed."

So the man went and brought the sheep inside with the hens. A week later, he went back to see the wise man and complained, "Please help me, wise man. My life is horrible. We can't sleep nor talk to each other, and the house stinks. Please help!"

The sage said, "All right, next week, take all the animals out."

And so he did. A week later, he went back to visit the sage. The sage asked him, "How is your life now?"

The man said, "Wonderful! The house is big, it smells good, we're sleeping soundly and we can hear each other. My life was good, but I didn't know it!"

***When we get used to our blessings, we lose sense of them and forget to be thankful, which may cause us to complain.***

When we get used to our blessings, we lose sense of them and forget to be thankful, which may cause us to complain, disregarding these blessings. In turn, our happiness level will drop. "Yet only a few of My worshippers are thankful." We lose sense of the gifts that are health, family, friends, safety, food, work, school, the janitor, our hearing, our sight, cool water, leisure time. Train yourself every day to remember these blessings; feel the praise in your prayers; when you see your children, thank God for their presence in your life; when you go to work, thank God for earning a living; when you eat, thank God for the gift of food; when you drink, thank God for the gift of water. Remember that thanksgiving is favoured by the Merciful: "God will be pleased with the worshipper who praises Him when he eats and praises Him when he drinks." Likewise, praise preserves blessings, and even multiplies them: "If you give thanks, I will give you more." You may have heard the story of the boy who went into the operation room to get his knee removed because of a tumour. But when he awoke, his knee was still there and the doctor told him they had misdiagnosed him. Later on, the boy shared, "Every morning, I look at my knee and thank God for his blessings." Ask yourself: how many blessings have you forgotten and neglected to be thankful for?

Abu Hurairah (may God be pleased with him) reported: "The Prophet (praise be upon him) said, 'By the One in Whose hand is my soul! This is among the favours which you shall be asked about on the Day of Judgement. Cool shade, tasty ripe dates and cool water'."

> *Praise be to God, the highest of praise... and thanks be to God before and after.*
> *Praise be to God for hearing and sight... Praise be to God for mind and body.*
> *Praise be to God for my leg and my foot... Praise be to God for my shoulder and for my hand.*
> *Praise be to God for my heart and my lungs... Praise be to God for my kidneys and my liver.*
> *Praise be to God for my mother and my father... and praise be to God for this worshipper's sisters.*
> *Praise be to God in secret and in public... Praise be to God in my sorrow and in my happiness.*
> *Praise be to God for what I know... and praise be to God for what I don't.*
> *Praise be to God, whose virtues prevail... and whose blessings defy logic.*
> *Praise be to God, followed by thanksgiving... Praise be to God for my thanks and for my praise.*

## What should I do?

- Monthly letter of gratitude: It has been found that writing a thank-you letter to others increases your happiness. So, every month, pick a person who has merit in your life: a relative, a friend, a co-worker, a teacher, a sheikh, a doctor, a worker. Tell him directly or write him a letter of thanks, appreciation and prayer, sharing your gratitude for what he gave you. It doesn't have to be sophisticated or eloquent, just write straight from the heart.
- Every weekend, write down 3 good things that happened to you that week, and why. For example:

| What happened | Why |
| --- | --- |
| I went out to dinner with my husband. | Because he wants me to feel his love, because he wanted me to rest on that day. |
| I met with a friend. | It was a pleasant encounter, we had lovely conversations… |

Writing down three good things and the reason behind them every week will help you become aware of your blessings. It will also bring you closer to others because you will pay attention to things that used to go unnoticed.

- During this week, start and end your day by praising God and thanking Him for the gift of life. Sense the value of life, of living a new day full of achievements and revelations. Thank the people in your life (your parents, friends, co-workers; anyone who did you a favour). Repeat the morning and evening Remembrances and meditate on them. (Praise is to God Who has given us life after taking it from us, and unto Him is the Resurrection.)
- (O God! Whatever favour has come to me, it comes from Thee alone Who has no partner; to Thee praise is due and thanksgiving) If you do this exercise, within a few days you will feel a strange new strength that makes you happier and more at ease.

## Scientific study:

The study on the health benefits of gratitude by Dr Robert Emmon and his research team at the University of California.

### What should I read?
*Gratitude: A Way of Life*, by Louise L. Hay.

# LIVE YOUR FEELINGS: WONDER, INSPIRATION

43. Be Amazed, Don't Be Rigid
44. Anything Can Inspire You
45. Fivefold Inspiration

# Be Amazed, Don't Be Rigid

Wonder is the spontaneous positive feeling we get when we encounter something awe-inspiring – whether in nature, ourselves, others, or in something man-made.

Amazement works in a miraculous and quick way, turning our focus away from any negative feelings. It expands our mind and opens us up to the immensity of the outside world.

You might be surprised to know that feelings of awe and wonder don't just increase your happiness level and reduce psychological stress: their benefits extend to your physical health.

A study on awe and inflammations, conducted by Jennifer Stellar at UC Berkeley, linked positive emotions – especially awe – with lower levels of a marker called "Interleukin 6". This boosts immunity, limits the gravity of bodily wounds and reduces stress and pain. Conversely, negative feelings increase this marker. So, if you see something that pleases or astonishes you, don't be rigid, rather say wholeheartedly, "Glory to God," and you will feel the effect of these words on your feelings and your health.

*Wonder motivated many successful people and inventors, making them think, or innovate, or increase their ambition and drive.*

Wonder isn't related to visual acuity or accuracy of sight. It's mainly about you feeling the world around you through observation, contemplation and mindfulness. Wonder increases your insight and expands your vision.

Sight isn't the only sense you can use to be amazed when feeling the world around you. Any God-given sense can help you be in awe of what you hear, taste, smell or touch.

Wonder is an innate feeling that we were born with, but many lose it along the way, with the hustle and bustle of life. You can learn about wonder by observing children because a child is easily amazed. Indeed, the simplest things like a rock, an ant carrying a grain, or even a cat playing with its kitten can amaze and move a child, who finds in it a new and exciting experience, which he enjoys with all his senses. Adults, however, don't see anything exciting or strange in these experiences, since they're governed by rigidity. And it's worth noting that many innovations and inventions came as a result of observing nature, animals and plants with an avid, amazed spirit:

- The best swimsuits are made of a material similar to the skin of a shark, whose characteristics make it the fastest swimmer among marine animals
- The millions of microscopic thorns covering the lotus flower protect it from dirt and water drops, thus wholly cleaning its leaves. Realizing this, a company manufactured a coating with microscopic nodules on the outside that prevent dirt or water particles from sticking to a surface. NASA also used this idea while making its space suits, to prevent bacteria from sticking to them
- Shinkansen bullet train: Japan is one of the first

countries to imitate nature (following the approach of innovations inspired by nature). In order to mitigate the noisy sound of high-speed trains, Japanese engineers were inspired by the well-known kingfisher (a bird that can penetrate the surface of the water with its thin beak without causing any ripples) to mask the noise of the train

➤ Researchers at the University of Leeds in Great Britain drew inspiration from the ultrasonic waves that bats emit to find prey. They designed walking sticks based on ultrasonic sounds emanating from inanimate objects, which humans can't hear, in an attempt to help the blind and visually impaired

Hence, wonder doesn't just improve our happiness level and health. If you read the biography of someone successful, or an inventor, you will find that something amazed them and made them think, or innovate, or increase their ambition and drive. Wonder is a spark that ignites the soul and pushes it to explore more!

Wasn't it the awe that famous journalist Daoud Al Sharyan felt when he travelled to the city of Al-Ahsa and watched television for the first time in his life, that instilled the love of media in him, thus turning him into a star in the field?

Wasn't the wonder that struck Abdallah bin Yahya Al-Mouallimi – famous Saudi diplomat and permanent representative of the Kingdom of Saudi Arabia to the United Nations – when he saw international flags in a gift that his father gave him as a child, the reason for his venture into politics and international affairs?

When you let wonder into your life, it will change it, leading you to contemplate the meaning behind things and your surroundings – from people to nature and heavenly verses. You will also be in awe of things that used to pass you by. Even the way you read the Quran will change. When you read the Quran, live with its verses and stop to contemplate a verse, a word or a meaning that struck you. You will live happier moments with this verse and discover new truths, as if reading it for the first time!

You may wonder, "How do I achieve amazement in my life? How do I train myself to feel wonder?"

Wonder is everywhere around us. The closer you look, the more astonished you will be. There is an abundance of amazing things: the sea, the magnificent desert and its sand, the movements of a new-born, melodious birdsong, the universe, the sophistication of outer space and the beauty of its riches, the sound of rain drops falling, the big, tall mountains, sunset, birds soaring in the sky, living creatures of all kinds, shapes and forms, the performance of outstanding athletes, the variety of plants…

***Wonder is in us and all around us. It's free and doesn't require travelling to specific places.***

Once, I even witnessed a man from Oman contemplating and talking about the wonders of a watermelon, in an amazing way I had never thought of before. He said, "This fruit is one of God's miracles! It's solid water that melts in your mouth. Even more, it's delicious as honey, and the most amazing thing is that it's protected by a coloured shell on every side." God Almighty doesn't just look after your sense of taste, but that of sight as well. Then God inspires you, as if saying, "Worshipper, if you like this product, I put its raw material, the seed, inside it. And remember, O Worshipper, that if you tried to eat the soil in which this seed grew, the bacteria present in this soil would kill you, but O Worshipper, I protected the seed for you and delivered it to you, and you happily ate it. So thank me for it."

Wonder is in us and all around us. It's free and doesn't require travelling to specific places, nor a study in a lab. You don't need to be a scientist or a specialist to have these positive feelings. If you look closely and meditate, you can see something that amazes you, makes you happy and increases your success and your faith every day.

In conclusion, wonder leads to exploration, research and innovation, as well as a stronger faith. Wonder makes us humbler, because when we feel awe, we realise the Creator's greatness, strength, and power; that He is greater than anything, and that creatures can't compare to Him. (Say: "Behold all that is in the heavens and on earth; but neither signs nor warnings profit those who will not believe.") Wonder increases our happiness level.

*The horizon is full of God's miracles, perhaps the least of which would guide you to Him.*
*Perhaps whichever of His miracles fills your soul is a wonder, if your eyes were to see it.*
*And the universe is full of secrets, which you couldn't explain if you tried.*
*Rather, ask the blind walking freely among the crowd, Who guides your steps?*
*Ask the foetus living in isolation, without shepherd nor pasture, Who watches over you?*

*Ask the new-born, crying and sobbing at birth, What made you cry?*
*And if you see a snake spitting out its venom, ask it, Who filled you with poison?*
*And ask it, How do you live and survive, O Snake, with a mouth full of poison?*
*And ask the bellies of the bees, How did you gather honeycomb, and ask the honeycomb, Who sweetened you?*
*Rather, ask filtered milk that was between blood and excrement, What cleared you up?*
*And if you see the living coming out of the folds of the dead, ask him, Who, O Living One, revived you?*
*Tell the plant that dries up after commitment and care, Who brought drought upon you?*
*And if you see a plant growing by itself in the desert, ask it, Who made you grow?*
*And if you see the full moon appear, casting its light, ask it, Who captured you?*
*And ask the rays of sun, reaching us even though they're the farthest from us, Who drew you near?*
*Ask the bitter fruit, Who fed you, among all other fruits, bitterness?*
*And if you see palm trees with split stems, ask them, O Palm Tress, Who split your stems?*
*And if you see a burning fire, ask its flames, Who stoked you?*
*And if you see the fragrant mountain that reaches the clouds, ask it, Who anchored you?*
*And if you see a rock bursting with water, ask it, Who cracked your smooth surface with water?*
*And if you see a river with fresh water running through it, ask it, Who made you flow?*

*And if you see the sea prevail with its briny water, ask it, Who made you prevail?*
*And if you see the night veiled in darkness, ask it, O Night, Who wove your darkness?*
*And if you see the morning dawn with laughter, ask it, O Morning, Who made you laugh?*
*Those of His miracles filling the universe will answer, a true wonder if your eyes could see.*
*Praise be to You, God, You alone, and no one but You.*
*O Springer of fragrant flowers, he who supplicated and prayed never failed.*
*O Mover of sweet, dewy rivers, he who supplicated and prayed never failed.*

# Anything Can Inspire You

When we see others surpass their limits and achieve their life ambitions, when we see how they react to the difficulties and obstacles they face, it inspires us and increases our drive to realise our own dreams.

*Inspiration is an important positive feeling because it pushes you to learn from people and circumstances and makes you strive for achievements.*

Inspiration is an important positive feeling because it pushes you to learn from people and circumstances and makes you strive for achievements. It also breaks the barrier of rigidity and despair that sometimes seep into the soul. Inspiration is a positive feeling that raises our happiness level.

In primary school, we read a story about Ahmad, the lazy student who would easily get bored and stop studying. One day, Ahmad was leaning on a tree branch when he saw an ant trying to carry a grain up to her anthill in the tree, in preparation for winter. The ant went up, then a few steps later, fell down the tree along with the grain.

Unphased, the ant picked up the grain and started climbing again. A few steps later, she fell down once more. Ahmad was watching all this intently. After a few tries, the ant was finally able to reach its home with the grain. The ant's many attempts and its unflinching patience inspired

Ahmad, whose lived changed henceforth.

Look around you and you will see inspiring people everywhere! Find inspiration in their stories, and contemplate

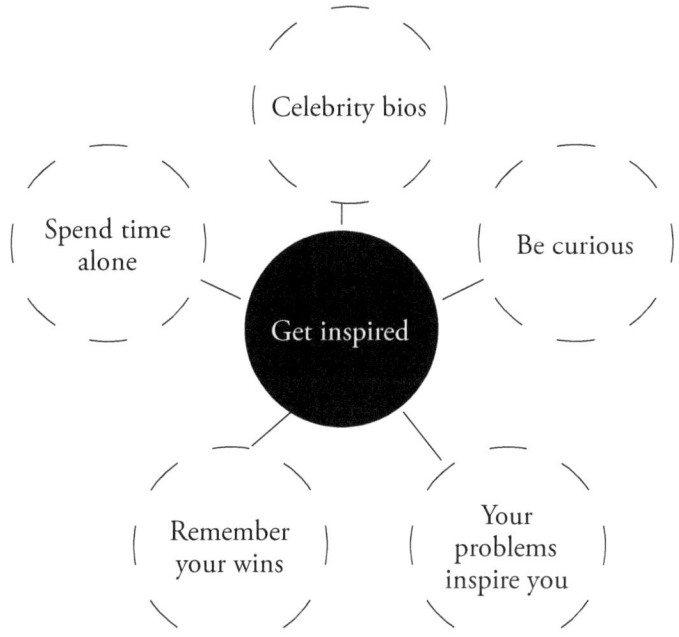

their behaviour. People, things and events in our life and around us, even problems, are a source of inspiration, on one condition: to look with eyes that seek knowledge and inspiration. Your father, your mother, your teacher, a baby, a street sweeper, the problems you face: they can all illuminate your path, or change your perspective, or instil happiness within you.

When I travelled to Cairo, I made it a point to always take a cab and listen to its driver: his life story, the problems he faced, his circumstances. Their stories inspired me and changed my outlook on so many things in life. Small problems stopped bothering me, because I realized that there are much bigger ones than those I faced. Indeed, one driver worked 14 hours a day, only getting out of his car when his legs fell asleep. Another started working at 16, when his father became terminally ill, forcing him to quit school to provide for his family. Another one couldn't stop working despite a spine injury, or he would end up homeless! I started appreciating the smallest blessings and enjoying the simplest things that I didn't use to pay attention to. For I had learned that there are people who work twice as much as me and have real problems and still they didn't give up, or become consumed by fear and worry.

# Fivefold Inspiration

- **Read celebrity bios:** The biographies of the successful and the great are fun and exciting to read. What's more, they offer you the gist of these personalities' experiences and the essence of their struggles, recounting the obstacles and challenges they faced as well as how they dealt with them. You will surely find something in their experiences that speaks to you, inspires you and lights your way. Call them "My heroes", make a list of them and study their life. Search for their interviews, read their biographies and meditate on the hardships they went through and their secrets for achieving their goals. Did they write any books you can read? Can you reach out to them? Some old books: Portraits from the Lives of the Companions and The Patience of the Pious Predecessors in Seeking Knowledge; and some new ones: Immortal Geniuses (Dar Al-sharq Al Arabi) and Do Not Despair, as well as the show Minal Sefer (From Scratch), and many more.

  It doesn't have to be someone famous. Become inspired by learning about the experience of people who accomplished goals similar to yours. You undoubtedly know someone who lost weight, got a masters' degree in a field you like, went through an experience or accomplished something at work. Don't hesitate: get in touch with them and get inspired. I attended a course on the concept of "quality" with an expert from the United Nations, during which one of the attendees asked him, "How did you get to this point?" The doctor had an answer that truly inspired me. He said, "Even when I'm afraid of a railway, I reach its end." Meaning, I don't give up easily. Words that inspired me a great deal.

➤ **Be curious:** Einstein said, "I have no special talent. I am only passionately curious." Next time you see something that catches your eye, don't just watch. Be curious, try to research and learn, because curiosity is an unquenchable desire and an insatiable appetite.

*Problems aren't intrinsically bad. They can even have positive aspects, but this depends on your focus, your decisions and the way you look at them.*

➤ **Your problems and circumstances:** Problems aren't intrinsically bad. They can even have positive aspects, since rough circumstances can teach and inspire you. As the owner of one of the most famous fast food chains says, "Failed projects have taught and inspired me more than successful ones." When things are going well, no one pays attention to them! People stop looking for better. Whereas problems can sometimes reveal genius ideas, but this depends on your focus, your decisions and the way you look at them. For instance, Hadeel got diabetes at age 7; she developed a watch that measures sugar levels in the body and pumps insulin into it. When asked, "How did you achieve this feat?" the little inventor said, "This idea was inspired by my illness."

And this other person who couldn't start his car for six hours and couldn't find any help. If he had spent that time blaming circumstances and people for not helping him, or the civil defence for being late, we would have been filled with rage and distress. But he stopped to calmly assess the situation and that's when inspiration struck! Thus, the idea to make a mobile app for roadside assistance was born. Indeed, Al-Suhaibani created the "Morni" application, which is worth nearly 100 million riyals. Don't be alarmed by problems. Rather, accept them and ask yourself: "What can this problem inspire in me and how can I learn from it?" Happy people turn their wounds into wisdom and use their failures to catapult them to success.

***Never underestimate your abilities.***
***They're a part of you. You have soared before,***
***and you will again.***

➤ **Remember your wins:** Sometimes, you have to be your own biggest inspiration! Use this trick whenever you feel weak, and need to overcome a challenge. Imagine you're going through a rough patch, or having problems in a relationship. Then, you should try to remember a similar past situation that you overcame. Meditate on it, and you will notice inspiration seep through you and peace flow in you. Remind yourself of the times you survived tough situations and insurmountable obstacles and were surprised with yourself and your ability to win. Never underestimate your abilities. They're a part of you. You have soared before and you will again. Most problems can be solved within you; all you need is the right incentive to regain your strength.

- **Spend time alone:** Feeling stressed day in and day out because of work, family, the responsibility of the family budget and tense relationships can backfire on you, weakening your inner strength. That's why it's hard for inspiration to strike when you're stressed, tired, or preoccupied. It's beneficial to set aside ten minutes every day to be alone with yourself and meditate. Calm, contemplative thinking will clear your mind and help you ponder the challenges facing you, or the opportunities you're offered. This solitude will increase your creative spirit and provide a comfortable and safe haven for you to think calmly, so you will be able to think about challenges more wisely. When you calm your mind, move away from what confuses you and listen to your inner voice, your thoughts will be more balanced, wiser and more inspiring.

- **Live your feelings:** Live the feelings of inspiration throughout your day. Observe nature and the creatures around you. Share your observations with others. Share them on social media; inspire others; ask your family and your children what they can learn from this or that creature. Live the feelings of inspiration throughout your day, contemplate the stories of the successful, and share them with your family and friends... Explore and be curious. Don't stand helpless in front of a problem you're facing, but ask yourself: "What does this problem teach me?" Remember positive past experiences and victories and how you overcame obstacles. Have a private session with yourself, in which you renew your energy and listen to your inner voice.

# LIVE YOUR FEELINGS, BE OPTIMISTIC

46. Optimism
47. Optimists
48. Why Be Optimistic?
49. The Optimism Blend
50. Obstacles to Optimism
51. Happy Thoughts

# Optimism

"Then He made the path easy for him." Ease is the essence of life. As for hardships, they're only temporary, and will pass. Always hope for the best and you will achieve it. For your trust in God will only bear good fruit.

**That's what happened**
Researchers put a barracuda fish and a small fish in a tank. It's known that barracudas are ferocious predatory fish with a strong jaw. They even prey on each other if they don't find something else to eat! The barracuda usually devours small fish at lightning speed. But in this experiment, the researchers placed an invisible glass separating the two fish. When the barracuda saw the little fish, it shot like an arrow to devour it but hit the invisible barrier and hurt its teeth. It kept trying but collided with the barrier every time and injured itself. In the end, the barracuda was convinced that it could not cross the barrier and that it would not be able to eat that fish. So, it gave up and stopped trying. Then the researchers quietly removed the glass barrier between the two fish and there was nothing separating them anymore. Oddly, the barracuda still didn't make any attempt to eat the small fish nor to cross the barrier. It stayed on its side, dying from hunger, even though its food was right there! What happened? The barracuda simply despaired; its thinking became limited and it became convinced that

it couldn't cross the barrier. All it was thinking was, "It's impossible! There's no way I can do it." What happened to that fish also happens to many of us: we hit a lot of roadblocks in life, so we stop trying and lose our optimism. Then we become depressed and lose our drive, even though we're close to achieving what we want. But the Prophet (peace be upon him) says: "God laughs at the despair of His worshippers, and how near change is. He looks at you despondent mortals; and He keeps laughing, knowing that your relief is near."

This is the biggest problem with pessimism: it takes away your drive in the face of life's challenges and undermines your hope for a better future. Optimism is indispensable for those who seek happiness. Optimism is one of the most important pillars of happiness, because hope drives optimists into action. Optimistic people also have the energy to beat challenges, as well as serenity and peace of mind. Optimism, and the belief that a better day will come and give us strength to overcome obstacles, make it easier to bear difficulties. If your financial situation worsens, or your life is woeful, or what you want isn't happening, or hateful and ill-intentioned people are oppressing you, or you're waiting for recovery or to obtain something… don't lose hope, and remember: Perhaps God is laughing, and perhaps relief is near. "With hardships comes ease."

*If your chest is tight, think about the pain, and God will open it up.*
*For hardship is coupled with ease, so don't despair.*

# Optimists

Optimists are usually happy and they're known for their ability to see the best in every situation. In their eyes, the world is full of opportunities, pleasures and wonders to be discovered. This mindset makes people love and welcome them because they spread happiness everywhere they go. Indeed, people prefer the company of optimists to that of pessimists and they're more inclined to listen to optimistic news and conversations, which bring them relief.

*Optimism doesn't mean that we always have to feel happy and joyous.*

Optimists generally believe that people and events are good in essence, and that most situations ultimately get resolved. Some optimists also think that, regardless of the outside world or a certain situation, people should choose to feel relief and fully benefit from its effects.

Optimism doesn't mean that we always have to feel happy and joyous. In fact, as we previously explained, trying to force yourself to be happy while going through a painful experience can be unhealthy. Optimism is to be aware, to identify your pessimistic thoughts as they emerge, and to ask yourself: "Is this pessimism realistic and justified? What can I do about it?"

Optimism is to recognise exaggerated negative thoughts and to replace them with positive ones.

Some people can't help putting pressure on themselves, feeling anxious about their present and fearful about their future. They insist on always wearing a cloak of pessimism, with or without reason! This may be due to their upbringing and the family in which they were raised, or the obstacles and circumstances they faced along the way, or their past, or their repeated failed attempts at something. But as we have already seen, these excuses don't justify pessimism. Regardless of the excuse, you can always change your life. Change starts in your own mind and the promises of God Almighty are the best reason to be optimistic: "Isn't morning near"; "Is not God enough for His servant"; "He does not despair of the spirit of God"; and so on.

# Why Be Optimistic?

> **The optimist achieves more:** An optimist believes that challenges and obstacles are temporary, that they will pass and that they're an intrinsic part of the solution. You never see him despair or get depressed, and he never quits. The pessimist, on the other hand, has a slogan: "Nothing will ever change, so why bother trying!" He usually despairs at the first rejection or breaks down in the face of the simplest problem. That's because he believes that his problems are permanent, everlasting and unsolvable, and that he is part of the problem. In a study conducted on a group of masters' graduates at Duke's Fuqua School of Business, optimists were hired faster and promoted quicker than pessimists.

*Hope is that inner voice that pushes you forward, telling you that tomorrow will be better and that God won't let your prayers and your hard work go to waste.*

When you reflect on the stories of successful, happy people around you, you will find a pattern: hope, ambition, generosity, failure, hard work, success, happiness. But what they all have in common is optimism and hope, without which nothing can ever be accomplished. A student who loses hope in passing his exams won't study; even if he does, he won't do it seriously. A wife who loses hope in fixing her relationship with her husband will despair and stop trying. An overweight person who loses hope in losing weight will start destroying his health and stop working out. And a patient who loses hopes in recovering will stop praying and looking for reasons to get better.

Hope is that inner voice that pushes you forward, telling you that tomorrow will be better and that God won't let your prayers and your hard work go to waste.

## *Optimists have longer, more satisfying relationships and marriages.*

› **The optimist has privileged relationships:** There is no doubt about that, since the optimist is upbeat, likes to discuss solutions and the good things that occur and smiles at everyone he meets. That's why people love him and love talking to him. Because he feels that the best is out there and he can achieve it. Likewise, the optimist naturally thinks that others are well-intentioned and treats them in good faith, unless proven otherwise! He makes excuses for them, sees the best in them and helps them see the positive in themselves. In a 2006 study published in the journal Personality and Social Relationships, it was confirmed that optimists have longer, more satisfying relationships and marriages.

## *An optimist has hope for the future and believes that life will turn out well.*

› **The optimist is healthier:** Optimism doesn't only

affect a person's mental and emotional health and his relationships; it also extends to his physical health. In fact, researchers at the University of Pittsburgh examined death rates and chronic health conditions among participants in the Women's Health Initiative study, which has been following more than 100,000 women ages 50 and over since 1994. As a result, optimistic women – who expect good rather than bad things to happen – were 14 percent less likely to die from any cause than pessimists and 30 percent less likely to die from heart disease after eight years of follow-up. Optimists were also less likely to have high blood pressure or diabetes or develop a habit of smoking. This isn't the product of divination or astrology; it's a scientific fact that optimism is one of the reasons for longevity, just as drugs lead to damaged brain cells – may God protect us all from evil. Because the optimist has hope for the future and believes that life will turn out well. Therefore, he gets excited about anything that benefits his health, such as sports, good relationships, a successful career and, in turn, all of these improve his health.

# The Optimism Blend

Optimism is a buzzword that we hear often but what is optimism, and how can you be optimistic? Studies have shown that realistic optimism is based on four things:

*The optimist believes he can change his life for the better.*
*Surrendering to circumstances is the enemy of success.*

1. The pessimist believes he is the reason behind all his problems, circumstances, misfortunes and mistakes; anything he does will always yield terrible results. The realistic optimist, however, believes he might be responsible for some of his problems but not for every bad thing in his life! Indeed, everything that happens to us is part of God's will and plan. We should take responsibility for the things we do that can be fixed but not every problem is on us. Hence, the optimist believes he can change his life for the better and that surrendering to circumstances is the enemy of success.

Pessimism often manifests itself as discouraging thoughts:
X My life won't get better.
X What I want won't happen.
X I ruined everything.
X I always bring problems on myself.

Remember that every thought you believe affects your whole life and repeating these negative expressions to yourself will only increase the negative things in your life and discourage you from acting. Therefore, believe that you're a wonderful person instead of putting yourself down and blaming yourself because that would neither make you happy nor improve your life! Self-flagellation would turn your life into a hard, painful experience, with no room for change and improvement.

### *The pessimist believes that bad circumstances are permanent, that things never change and that life doesn't get better.*

2. Won't, never, always: these are words that the pessimist uses to describe his circumstances, since he believes that bad circumstances are permanent, that things never change and that life doesn't get better. For his part, the realistic optimist avoids generalisations and knows that, although circumstances are currently bad, they won't always stay that way. Thus, optimism makes everything better. The problems and obstacles facing me won't last, for happiness and ease are the essence of life. If a negative person fails, he loses his self-confidence, blowing his failure out of proportion and undermining his past success, then he gives up trying. As for the positive person, he considers

it a teachable moment and, armed with optimism, he works on improving his methods.

At one point or another, we all tried to quit bad habits, failed repeatedly, then gave up. We tried to better ourselves then, after a few failed attempts, simply stopped trying. We tried to achieve some goals but weren't successful right away, so we slacked off; we prayed to God and He didn't answer, so we stopped praying; we tried to get a promotion or a job, or start a new relationship, and our attempts were unsuccessful.

How do you react to such obstacles and challenges? If you're a pessimist – God forbid – you will lose hope. Your pessimism will stop you from giving it another shot and you will despair, which will keep you from getting what you want in life. Whereas if you're an optimist, you will know that not all your attempts will yield the desired results. It's okay to be upset sometimes! But giving up is not an option, as you believe that these failed attempts are a test from God. Will you despair and give up, or will you hold on to your optimism, hard work and drive, confident that God will give you what you desire? So don't let unsuccessful attempts or failed experiences bring you down, for God might erase them and give you what you want on the next try. And remember that every unsuccessful attempt brings you closer to your goal. Only the faithless despair of the spirit of God. When faced with obstacles, double your efforts; only fighters achieve success. Politician Ali Al-Naimi started out as a reporter, billionaire Saleh Al Rajhi was a mere banker at first and international designer Siraj Sanad – who designed the Beijing Olympics three times – used to be a gas station attendant. Similarly, Saleh Kamel began his career as a reviewer for government auditors, Rafic Hariri used to pick citrus fruits and Dr Abdullah Al-Fawzan was employed by a family as a driver. What did these successful people have during hard times? Faith in God and hope, of course. Furthermore, each one of them believed that his problems and circumstances were temporary and that tomorrow will be better.

> ***Always remind yourself that you deserve a better life and treat yourself with respect, regardless of your charisma, your wealth and your intelligence.***

3. The pessimist falls into a trap that destroys him and his self-confidence, because he believes that he doesn't deserve happiness, success or respect, that some job is out of his league and that he can't lead a decent and happy life, nor be associated with distinguished people, because he is inferior to them! These thoughts bring about despair and depression and make his life slowly crumble. The third pillar of optimism is believing that you deserve everything good in life.

Always remind yourself that you deserve a better life, just like any human being. Treat yourself with respect, regardless of your charisma, your wealth and your intelligence. You deserve it for one simple reason: you're human. This way of thinking should come to you as naturally as needing food to survive. Appreciate yourself, for people treat you the way you treat yourself! And remember that your existence has value and purpose; don't waste it! Sometimes, such negative thoughts are planted by other people, so never pay attention to any words that undermine you or your abilities.

Someone once told a beautiful story: "One day, my boss came to me upset, saying, 'You're not fit for this job!

It's too big for you.' And indeed, he transferred me to a lesser position with an inferior salary. I felt so small and begrudgingly started the new position. I worked there for two years, believing my boss's statement that I don't deserve a better position! Two years later, the company went bankrupt. While I was looking for a new job, I found an ad for a company who had a mandatory aptitude test before any new hire. I took said test, then, to my surprise, the HR manager called me curiously wondering, 'Why did you apply for a lesser position, when you got the best score on the aptitude test and were the best in the personal interview?' And indeed, I was appointed to a good position and today I am one of their best employees."

***On your journey to happiness, you will face circumstances and challenges. Some will tell you that you can't make it and others will envy you because you found your path in life.***

On your journey to happiness, you will face circumstances and challenges. Some will tell you that you can't make it, that you're not worthy, or that you won't get what you want! And others will envy you because you found your path in life. Don't mind them; rather, be optimistic and have faith in God and that tomorrow will be better. Understand their feelings and ignore them; don't let them interrupt your journey.

4. Optimists look for the bright side, even in unwanted circumstances, events and situations, which makes them happier and more optimistic. Several studies indicate that the mind tends to look for the negative. For instance, if you

pass by a tall, beautiful building with hundreds of lovely blue windows and just a single broken one, your eyes will be drawn to that window. Your thoughts will then revolve around the reason for its state and why no one has repaired it. Thus, you will automatically ignore the beauty of that building, because of one window. The natural inclination of the mind is to focus on what is going wrong in our lives, rather than what is going well. When something bad happens, look for the bright side; it will help you overcome difficult situations and make you more optimistic. It will also reduce anxiety and depression and help develop different aspects of your life. Practise this in the coming weeks. If your salary is late, the bright side is that you still have a job; if one of your parents is angry with you, the bright side is that they're still alive and you can still make things right; if you get stuck in traffic, the bright side is that you own a car, and can also listen to educational programs while you wait. There are people who memorized the Quran, others who listened to hundreds of lesson; there is even a pilot who took advantage of the long travel hours to read many books; and even wrote some! All this because he looked for the bright side. Daoud Al Sharyan recounts how, when he got colon cancer, he underwent a surgery and as a result, had a tube installed in his colon, which cut him off from the outside world for a while. Yet, this event had many bright sides: "I started sleeping early, my health improved, I had free time to read and write, my relationship with my family improved." So, train yourself in the coming weeks to see the bright side, and you will be amazed at how much happier and more optimistic you have become.

# Obstacles to Optimism

As the saying goes, "Wash your cup before filling it and untie the strings before setting off." And like Ibn al-Qayyim says, "Purification before beautification." It's important for you to know that there are obstacles to optimism, which you have to deal with before you can journey into the world of optimists.

**What are you watching?**
What is shown in the media and what are the top news on satellite channels?

Most breaking news involve wars, explosions, terrorism, murder, hate and scandals. These are the main interests of newscasts and popular online news sites: negative news that spread frustration and pessimism. Try visiting the website of an online newspaper or watching the news on a TV channel. What follows is an example of the top news in an online newspaper today:

- **A corpse, a gas tank and a letter:** Al-Qunfudhah security is investigating the mystery of a death
- **Suspicious bag gets terminal at Manchester Airport evacuated**
- **Watch the moment a Russian nuclear missile exploded, with disastrous results**
- **Tragedy:** a disabled Indian woman was beaten to death for reasons unknown

▸ **A fatal mistake:** watch what a Lebanese groom did to his wedding photographer!

You will find that most news focus on problems, wars and violence. These newspapers and channels don't focus, for example, on millions of successful marriages, billions of happy families, billions of safe and beautiful places around the world, billions of calm, uneventful flights.

Why does the media spread bad news? Because they're the most watched and followed.

For God's sake, how can one become positive when addicted to this type of news?!

When watching such news becomes a daily meal, you will drain your positive feelings and your happiness level will plummet. You will become frustrated and pessimistic about the future and you will think that the whole society is rotten and corrupt. And you'll get what you focus on.

*If you focus on your fears, you would be feeding them and they will increase. Starve them in order to vanquish them.*

Try discussing optimism with someone addicted to the news and to websites that spread negative information. He will surely mock you and tell you that every home has problems, that the world is heading towards a disaster, war, economic collapse and that society has become corrupt! If you focus on your fears, you feed them and they increase. Starve them in order to vanquish them. Don't spare them any time or energy; don't give them ammunition with horror movies or negative news. Hence, limit your exposure to bad news as well as spreading them. Listen to what brings you comfort instead and your life will be more peaceful. And remember: The fear in your heart is like grass in soil: it will only grow if you water and feed it. So stop watering and it will dry up and weaken.

I found these wise words in the book Live Life Like Never Before:
*"I was afraid of failure*
*Until I realised I only fail when I don't try*
*I was afraid of success*
*Until I realised that I should keep trying until I achieve happiness*
*I was afraid of people's opinions*
*Until I learned that people have opinions of me no matter what I do*
*I was afraid of rejection*
*Until I learned to believe in myself*
*I was afraid of pain*
*Until I learned that it is necessary for growth"*

## What are you thinking about?
Self-talk plays a big part in planting the seeds of optimism or pessimism. If you are constantly beating yourself up and scolding yourself, always expecting the worst, or over-judging others, it will increase your pessimism. Why did I do this? Why didn't I do that? I'm to blame for all my problems! I will never have a successful future! This person is full of flaws! Why did I say these words? What did so-and-so mean by this gesture?

## OBSTACLES TO OPTIMISM

***Don't criticize yourself, blame circumstances and people, or expect bad news, because what you're worried about may never happen.***

Everybody makes mistakes. But some don't mind making them, while others are afraid of making mistakes and berate and scold themselves when they do, and others still are obsessed with monitoring other people's mistakes. Balance is key. We should do our best to avoid mistakes and learn from the ones we make, instead of overly blaming ourselves for making them. Indeed, we did the best we could with the resources we had. And you should know that everyone who achieved a high rank made mistakes along the way. Take Ali Al-Qahtani: he was a victim of embezzlement at the start of his career, but it taught him a lesson that pushed him forward. Likewise, Youssef Al-Dawood failed in his bakery project and made serious mistakes. So, he put the appropriate amount of blame on himself, learned from his mistake, then embarked on a journey towards happiness and success. Thus, don't criticise yourself, blame circumstances and people, or expect bad news. What you're worried about may never happen. Expecting the worst and worrying about things that may or may not happen wastes your energy and imprisons you in a cycle of negative thinking.

***If you pay too much attention to a negative person, he may unintentionally plant poisonous thoughts in your mind.***

**Who are you befriending?**
There was a street vendor who used to sell pastries. He had poor hearing and eyesight, so he couldn't follow the news and wasn't up to date at all. Since he was extremely skilled in pastry-making, his sales increased and he was able to buy a brand-new shop with a big sign. He also started selling juice along with pastries. With the increase in sales, he recruited his son, who was a college student. After a short while, his son told him, "Father, you don't follow the news. The country's economic situation is bad, unemployment is on the rise and there's a great recession coming!" Fear and worry started seeping into the vendor's soul and he thought to himself, "My son follows the news and goes to college. Surely, he knows better than I do." After which, he decided to make fewer pastries and stop selling juice. He also took down the sign. With time, the sales decreased considerably. Until one day, the vendor turned to his son and said, "You were right, Son, the great recession is here!"

If you pay too much attention to a negative person, he may unintentionally plant poisonous thoughts in your mind. "The economy is bad; society is corrupt; the current situation is catastrophic; you won't achieve what you want!" These thoughts will be stored in your brain. With time, their effects will start showing: They will demoralise you, weaken your self-confidence and make your view of yourself and the world bleak. Then you'll start to expect the worst, thus succumbing to depression and isolation. So, always ignore negative people, focusing on your life and goals instead. Negative people can paint the worst picture of the world and it still wouldn't be worse than the situation Ibrahim put his wife in: he left her in an uncultivable valley and still, she exclaimed, "God will not neglect us."

*Be optimistic, for the morning will come brightly… after a dark night*
*And God will bless you, so do not despair… nor waste your life in grief*
*Be confident, be faithful and true… Be resilient, and ever smiling*
*Be like a fragrant aroma, filling others with its scent… Be the flame of faith in the dark*

# Happy Thoughts

- Everything has a special flavour, even darkness, silence, and me. I have learned to be happy regardless of the situation I'm in
- Every day brings a new opportunity, a new attempt, a new experience. I can always change my life. And I can have a new start every day
- It's always better to look forwards rather than back
- Don't despair; the last key in a bunch is often the one that opens the door
- People become old when they choose excuses over hope
- Tomorrow will be better and brighter and I am now enjoying the present moment.
- Whatever I'm going through, as long as I'm alive I know that I will get a second, third, fourth chance, and more
- Every difficulty will be easy to deal with if you rely on God
- The story doesn't end when I lose, but when I don't do anything about it except complain
- Tomorrow is a better day. This is what hopes tells us and this is what God says to us: "Now no person knows what delights of the eye are kept hidden (in reserve) for them."
- At the heart of every winter, there's a beating spring. And at the end of each night, there is a smiling dawn.

➤ Tomorrow: a new, beautiful life awaits me, with everything I want and love; for God is kind and generous.

## What should I do?

Live your feelings. Live the feelings of hope throughout your day.

- ☛ Leave past mistakes behind / don't blame yourself for what is done. When you find yourself thinking of a mistake or a bad experience, stop and ask yourself, "What can I learn from it?" Then go about your day
- ☛ Pay attention to what you watch this week. Limit newscasts as well as negative shows and series, which spread gloom, sadness, betrayal, and focus on problems. Watch programs that bring you happiness and make you optimistic
- ☛ When someone talks in a pessimistic way, be optimistic, radiate hope and remind him that with hardship comes ease
- ☛ Better yourself in an area or two of your life, because pessimism arises from helplessness and loss of control. Set a life goal or two and work towards them. This will help you regain your trust in your personal strength and your capacity to make changes to your everyday life
- ☛ Be at peace with your inner self. He who reconciles with himself before other people will have the spirit of optimism coursing through his body. If you catch yourself blaming yourself, stop right away and focus on what you can do. Remember, you only live once, so don't over-blame or criticise yourself, as it won't fix anything in your life

- Pay attention to your words and thoughts. If you find yourself stuck in negative generalisations, such as, "I won't accomplish… There's no way I can get… I can't recover… This boy is no good," quickly replace them with positive statements: "God will change circumstances for the better. With hardship comes ease. If I get sick, He will heal me. God will reform him."
- Smile often. Putting a smile on your face can make you feel happier and more optimistic about the present as well as the future
- In moments of frustration or apathy, remember your achievements and victories. These are rest areas that can strengthen you and make you more optimistic

**WHAT SHOULD I READ?**

*Don't Live Your Life In One Day*, by Johnny Ong.

# LIVE YOUR FEELINGS / PASSION

52. Your Passion
53. Passion Drives You Even in Moments of Weakness
54. From the Chicken Coop

# Your Passion

When you work towards your passion, you will do it more meticulously. Everything will come together in a beautiful, magical way, and everybody will help you.

**That's what happened**
In 1994, a boy in the 9th Grade enrolled on a training course in computers, which were far less popular then than today. He loved everything about the course, especially the machine itself, and he met other students. After the course ended, he kept studying on his own. Three years later, in 1997, while flipping through a newspaper, he read about something called the internet, and how this wonderous new web worked. Later on, he revealed: "This news shocked me and monopolized my thoughts, to the point that I couldn't sleep that night!

The next morning, I called one of the friends I had made three years earlier, during the course, asking him about this new 'internet'. He told me he was working at one of the first companies that provide a basic internet service. I visited the company headquarters, which only had two employees, and asked to join them. I was in high school at the time. They turned me down at first but I told them I would work for free, because my goal was to feed the passion within me.

They accepted my offer and I started working there.

## YOUR PASSION

Those were some of the happiest days of my life. A year later, I had gained excellent experience and imposed myself, so I told them I would start looking for a new job since I was now an experienced employee who wasn't getting paid. Here, they negotiated with me because I knew the ins and outs of the business and offered me a percentage of shares in exchange for staying, which I accepted. Merely a few months later, a big company made an offer to buy ours and my share amounted to a million riyals." Faisal Al-Khamissi then went on to create his own company, achieving success after success, until he built an empire worth over 800 million riyals.

What kept Faisal awake that night and what made him work for free? Your passion is something you do that makes you happy, even without getting paid. Having a passion means living a purposeful life.

# Passion Drives You Even in Moments of Weakness

Passion is an inspiring, exhilarating force that drives your life and your thoughts. It makes you look forward to the future and love your life, excitedly awaiting anything new in it. Passion gives your life meaning and allows you to accomplish a lot of tasks without getting bored. Passion is to love life and yourself. Passion is to love others, it's to discover your true life goals. It's real living, because when you discover your passion, you will love yourself, stand out from the crowd and achieve your goals.

*Passion energises you and increases your creativity. Indeed, a weak desire yields weak results.*

Passion is something you do that makes you happy. Everyone has their own passion. Positive passion fuels us to continue in our path and move forward. Passions vary, as everyone has their own, such as raising children, programming, painting, driving, teaching, flying, engineering and so on. Passion energizes you and increases your creativity. Indeed, a weak desire yields weak results and a weak fire generates little heat. The stronger your fire, the bigger your passion and your accomplishments.

Cooking might be a routine activity for some but those who are passionate about cooking enjoy it and its aromas, thus turning it into a source of happiness. Follow some celebrities or watch a cooking competition and you'll see the difference between those who cook out of necessity and those who cook out of passion! To better understand the connexion between passion and happiness, read these words by the most popular chef, Ali Youssef, who discovered his passion for cooking and has been working in this field for over 15 years: "The only thing that satiates my passion and brings me contentment is my live show, or interacting with my audience on social media and sharing my thoughts and cooking tips. I am happiest when communicating directly with my followers on Snapchat, getting questions or comments, and answering the public's inquiries…" Hence, anything you're passionate about will turn into creativity and happiness, no matter what.

***The passion that courses through your veins is a sign that you're following your destiny and looking for more.***

Passion pushes you to accomplish what you desire. It's the fuel that drives you forward, towards your goals. If you want something bad enough, you will find yourself pursuing it, and rushing to achieve it. As Omar bin Abdulaziz said, "I have an eager soul that, if given something, longs for more."

The passion that courses through your veins is a sign that you're following your destiny and looking for more. Passion is also an indicator of your quality of life and activity, no matter your age. As it has been said, "No one is old because he has lived for many years, but man is old when he abandons his goals and objectives. Years may affect your facial features, but giving up your enthusiasm and passion is what weakens our spirits; for passion is a very important thing."

Scientists couldn't figure out why some students – male and female – were dropping out of military school soon after enrolling, while others kept going diligently and steadily until graduation. Was it an individual's muscle power, his intelligence, his athletic skills? They finally discovered that the perseverance of some students had nothing to do with scientific knowledge, excellence or physical attributes. Rather, it lay in their "passion" for accomplishing these goals. This was the conclusion reached by the study, which was conducted by two researchers from West Point College, a third from the University of Pennsylvania and a fourth from the University of Michigan, USA.

Think about all the happy people you know: the successful; the achievers like athletes, scientists and businessmen; those who succeeded in building a happy family; those who excel at their job. What do all these people have in common? Without a doubt, the answer is: a tireless passion for what they do. And this – as the book The Success Factor states – is the ultimate success factor.

Has a mother with a passion for her family ever stopped raising her children? Has a business owner who is passionate about his trade ever abandoned it? Was there ever a teacher with a passion for his vocation who hated going to school? Was there ever a talented soccer player who quit in the middle of a game?

***If you suppress your passion for the things you love, you will grow indifferent towards everything.***

## PASSION DRIVES YOU EVEN IN MOMENTS OF WEAKNESS

These things rarely happen, because when you love something it stops being a chore and doing it makes you happy. You would even do it for free, like Faisal. Follow your passion, not money; because passion brings you happiness and money, whereas money doesn't get you passion!

If you suppress your passion for the things you love, you will grow indifferent towards everything, without exception. All you will do is sleep and watch your life events without any reaction. You will become lethargic and boredom will take over your life. When we lose passion, we lose our aim, then we lose our willingness to act, then success, happiness… everything! Keep in mind that you must nurture your passion in order for it to survive. Do what you love, so that you love what you do. Have a dream and strive to achieve it. Pick a skill and spend your life mastering it. Do all that you love and everything you do will raise you up and make you better.

# From the Chicken Coop

Hussein was living in Taif when he graduated high school. Like any student, he was confused about which college to attend and which path to follow. "Should I do as my parents told me, or go to the same college as my friends, or pick the one with the major I want, even if it doesn't offer a promising future?"

There were two main options, either the Air Force College, which offered a high salary during and after study, as well as fewer years of study; or Agricultural Engineering, which was what Hussein wanted to do, despite an uncertain future.

Hussein decided to follow his passion and go into Agricultural Engineering in Riyadh. In the last year of college, students had to pick a graduation project revolving around agriculture. Incidentally, one of Hussein's relatives owned a chicken coop in As-Sahba', a region fifty miles from Riyadh. Hussein did his project there, thus discovering chicken coops. After graduating, he started a government job in the municipality of Jeddah. Hussein didn't fit in at his job because he wasn't working in his field. He then contacted the relative who owned a chicken coop and agreed to work for him for the same salary. The work environment at the coop was tough and dirty, to the point that at the end of every work-day, Hussein would reek of chicken for hours. After two years of struggle and self-affirmation, Hussein moved on to a better job with a higher salary at a bigger poultry company. Five years later, famous businessman Saleh Kamel offered him ten times his current salary to run his agricultural investments and Hussein quickly started working for him. Five years later, he decided to open his own coops, which soon expanded until he owned coops in various countries. Why did Hussein Bahri choose difficulty over the temptations of the Air Force College? Why did he persevere in the face of challenges, leaving his family and his city, as well as the safety of government work? Why was he content with a lower salary and fewer benefits, working for a poultry company as a hangar supervisor, the lowest job in this field? Hussein didn't ask himself the wrong question: "What should I do to be rich?" Rather, he asked himself: "What should I do to feel alive, to leave my mark?"

Of course, passion was the answer, as it is the secret key to happiness and success. It's what pushes you to put all your energy into your goals and what keeps you going even when things are bad.

***Passion is the secret key to happiness and success and what pushes you to put all your energy into your goals.***

Hussein is a happy, well-balanced person, whose passion isn't reserved for his work. Indeed, he says he's convinced that a happy life is a balanced one. Which is why he is passionate about charitable work and organisations and has a passion for building his legacy like he built his life.

**WHAT SHOULD I DO?**
In order to find out what you're passionate about, here are some tips to discover your passion:
- ☛ Think of the things that make you happy
- ☛ Think of the activities you like to do
- ☛ Think about your values in life
- ☛ Think about yourself, and identify your strengths
- ☛ Think about yourself, and identify your weaknesses
- ☛ Think of the subjects you like to talk about
- ☛ Think of the people you wish to be like
- ☛ Think of the things you always dreamed about

**WHAT SHOULD I READ?**
*Grit: The Power of Passion and Perseverance*, by Angela Duckworth.

# YOUR PERSONAL STRENGTH

55. Don't Strain Your Eyes
56. The Negativity Bias
57. Thinking Traps: Generalisation, Omission, Distortion
58. The Positivity Seeker and the Negativity Seeker
59. Lean Towards Positivity
60. Minds Are Like Computers
61. The Present Moment Is the Key to Happiness
62. The Inner Mirror
63. The Self-Esteem Quartet
64. Cut the Imaginary Ropes

# Don't Strain Your Eyes

On any given day, if five good things and one bad thing were to happen to you, your mind would focus on the negative, thus keeping you from enjoying the day. Focusing on the negative obscures the beauty of life.

**That's what happened**
Two students at a Canadian school got a whacky idea. One night, they took three goats to school, unbeknownst to the principal and teachers. They wrote "Number 1" on the first goat, "Number 2" on the second, and "Number 4" on the third. Then they released the goats at the school and went home.

The next day, when they went to school, the principal, the teachers and the students were met with a surprising, strange smell – that of goat droppings, which were all over the school property. The principal was very upset, while employees started chasing after the goats. They managed to catch all three, after which one employee told the principal, "We caught all the goats, except one that's still missing. We found goats number 1, 2 and 4, but couldn't find goat number 3." The principal asked his employees to look again, and they did. They exhausted themselves looking everywhere for that goat, but of course, it was in vain. Indeed, they were looking for something that didn't exist; there was no goat number 3!

This is what happens to a lot of us, when we busy ourselves with things we lost and aren't part of our life anymore, over-think about what we don't have or a frivolous attitude, or focus on problems and horrors that might or might not occur. In so doing, we disturb our happiness and peace of mind, forgetting our goals and dreams. Our biggest concern becomes ruminating on our flaws, what we lack, and what frightens us – despite their insignificance in the bigger picture of our life.

This is called "the negativity bias", which is when negative events or feelings typically have a more significant impact on our psyche than positive ones, even when they are of equal proportion. This tendency exists in you, me and most humans. This is why it's important to be aware of it, and to catch ourselves when our thoughts start leaning towards negativity. The negativity bias may change your happiness into boredom and sadness, even if you were leading a good, happy life, because negative thoughts and rigidity overwhelm you and deplete your positive energy.

# The Negativity Bias

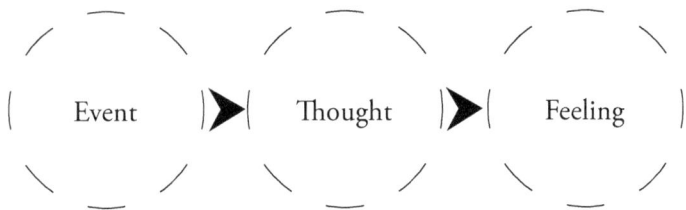

Were you ever in a similar situation?

**First situation:**
You had a wonderful gathering where you had a lovely talk with your family or friends. After leaving, suddenly and without any apparent reason you notice that you forgot everything good about the gathering. Instead, you started focusing on something someone said or a tiny negative situation that occurred.

**Second situation:**
You gave an excellent presentation and your explanation was clear. But there was a simple comment, or a normal mistake you let slip, and afterwards all you could remember from the presentation was that simple comment!

**Third situation:**

## THE NEGATIVITY BIAS

You have a wonderful relationship with a friend. Suddenly, he does something that doesn't sit well with you and that situation takes over your thoughts, poisoning your relationship in the days that follow.

This is exactly like looking for the missing goat: it's not very important, but it invades your thoughts and disturbs your life. This is the negativity bias, which is when our minds are influenced by and focus on the negative more than the positive.

If you let this way of thinking control you, it will harm you, affecting your life, your self-perception and your relationships, even the professional ones, badly.

You're not the only one with a negativity bias. On the contrary, it's something we all have in common. Still, you can reduce it, improve your life and elevate your thoughts.

One of the reasons behind this way of thinking is that our mind is trying to protect us. Consequently, it considers any negative event as a threat, even though it might not be one at all! Hence, our mind rushes to store any negative situation or event in the first second of its occurrence. Conversely, the mind needs ten seconds to store positive situations.

In addition, an important reason for our mind's negativity bias is wrong thinking, such as: generalization, omission and distortion, which I like to call thinking traps!

## Thinking Traps: Generalization, Omission, Distortion

Your thoughts are the starting point for your feelings. For instance, when you're in a hurry and witness an accident that stopped traffic, if you think about the injured and his family, you will feel compassion and sadness; if you think about the accident itself and how it's keeping you from work, you may feel angry and tense; and if you think that God made you late to keep you out of harm's way, you will feel relieved and grateful. So, if you want to change your feelings, your first mission is to examine your thoughts and the way you assess a situation, then re-evaluate said situation, challenge a negative thought, or replace it with a positive one. Sometimes, our "irrational" thinking – thinking in an inadequate, unwise way – is the reason behind our actions and behaviour. Indeed, there are thinking traps into which we fall and of which we must be aware.

*Check your entirely irrational thoughts and you'll see that they don't serve you, nor make you happy, nor help achieve your goals.*

If you have a job interview or an important meeting, you will feel stressed. Here, it's never right to address your feelings: "Don't be stressed, don't be scared." The right way to go is to check your thoughts. Our thoughts cause our feelings.

When you check your thoughts, you'll see that most of the time they are entirely irrational. They don't serve you, nor make you happy, nor help achieve your goals.

There was a man whose home was far away from his place of work. He grew tired of the distance, so he decided to sell his house and move closer to his job. He went to his friend – a businessman and marketing expert – and asked him to help write the "for sale" ad. The expert knew the house well, so he wrote a detailed description, highlighting the beautiful location, the large surface, and the lovely neighbours. He described the architectural design, then talked about the beautiful garden and all the available nearby services.

Once he was done, the expert read the ad to the home-owner, who listened intently, then said, "Please read it again!"

When he did, the owner exclaimed, "What a wonderful house!" Then he said smiling, "Please don't post the ad, my house isn't for sale!"

This man had ignored all of his house's features because he was focusing on a single flaw, which kept him from enjoying it and almost made him lose it. Don't let a negative situation blind you to your kind friends, your loving relatives, your job, your boss or anything beautiful in your life! Check your thoughts carefully and be more reasonable.

**The problem with negative generalization**
Negative generalization is one of the thinking traps that destroys happiness. It lies in the fact that when you face a problem, or don't get what you want, your thoughts tend

to generalize this negative event, applying it to all your life situations. Or they might blame your personality for the problem and blame you for what happened. The problem with negative generalization is that it exacerbates what happened to you to the point that you forget everything else. For example, if a husband is generally good to his wife but does her wrong one time and she says, "You've never been good to me," then she has fallen into this destructive trap. Therefore, it becomes a danger to her faith and her life.

Similarly, when you fail a test or a project and have thoughts like: "I will never succeed," then you are labelling yourself as a failure or an idiot, and feelings of weakness and surrender will seep into you. When you go through a bad situation with someone and you have thought of negative generalization, such as: "No one ever respects me. People are no good. You can't trust anyone. Nobody loves me…" you start losing your self-confidence and becoming overwhelmed by a negative perception of yourself as well as others. Then you'll feel afraid, or resent others and feel isolated from them.

Likewise, when you're giving a speech in front of a crowd and you notice someone busy or inattentive to your words, then you might have thought of negative generalization: "No one cares about what I have to say. It seems that I'm boring." Therefore, feelings of frustration and lack of enthusiasm start to creep in.

This way of thinking – negative generalization – is unreasonable and can spoil your happiness. Indeed, it's unreasonable to let one situation, event, person or reaction cause us all these feelings, making us judge ourselves and others!

THINKING TRAPS: GENERALIZATION, OMISSION, DISTORTION

***Being aware of your thoughts, then challenging and changing negative ones, will improve your feelings and your judgement.***

### Challenging negative generalization

It's very important to watch out for thinking traps. First, look at the situation from a distance instead of drowning in it; it will reduce the impact of your negative feelings. Then ask yourself: "What is the wrong thought that stirred up all these big negative feelings in me? Am I blowing the matter out of proportion? How can I challenge, change, or refute this thought?"

Being aware of your thoughts, then challenging and changing negative ones, will improve your feelings and your judgement. It's also a very important step towards eradicating negative thinking, then banishing these feelings that are hindering your happiness.

You can always challenge any negative situation, or re-evaluate it, or replace it with a more positive, optimistic situation and perspective.

- ☞ When you face a negative situation with a friend and you think something like: "This person is always hurting me," ask yourself first: "Is this thought reasonable? Am I blowing things out of proportion?" Then ask yourself a positive question that challenges this generalisation: "What are some of his positive attitudes? Does he really always hurt me?"
- ☞ When you fail a test and have a thought like: "I will never succeed. I can't catch a break," ask yourself: "Is this thought reasonable? Am I blowing things

out of proportion?" Then ask yourself a challenging question: "How many times have I succeeded in the past, and how many times did God give me a break?"

You can also re-evaluate any negative situation.

- ☞ If someone "gets distracted" while you're speaking, it doesn't mean that no one is paying attention. Every person has his circumstances and his interests and it's not your responsibility to draw everyone's attention, nor convince them, nor make them love or accept you. Rather, your responsibility is to give what you can.
- ☞ Debating your thoughts will challenge thinking traps, change your feelings, stop the negative energy that's draining your happiness and eliminate your rigidity. These inner discussions will also help you succeed in life because they bring you back to a reasonable, correct and rational way of thinking. As we have previously seen, negative feelings limit your options and reduce you to a fight-or-flight reaction. Conversely, positive feelings broaden your horizons, multiply your options and increase your flexibility in the face of negative situations. They also allow you to see the bigger picture, instead of drowning in a situation or event and generalizing it.

Negative thought + negative generalization = negative feelings

Negative thought + challenge and discussion + positive perspective = healthy positive feelings

# The Positivity Seeker and the Negativity Seeker

Life isn't all roses. Everyone experiences hurtful situations, painful circumstances and unfortunate events. Sometimes, we may be wronged by others. At such a time, you might think and wonder, "Why did so-and-so hurt me? Why did so-and-so wrong me? Why did the project fail? Why did I fall ill?"

When circumstances make you sad, angry and frustrated, remember that this won't benefit you. If you want to overcome circumstances and problems facing you, you have to grow stronger and change the way you handle them.

Your perspective plays a big part in your happiness or unhappiness, as well as in overcoming bad circumstances. Studies have confirmed that, when dealing with failure, difficulties and problems, people can be split into two categories:

| The seeker of advantages | The seeker of disadvantages |
|---|---|
| What I want may not happen but I can accomplish better things than what happened to me. Everything will be all right in the end. | What I didn't want happened and this is the way it will always be. My goals and wishes won't come true. Things will only get worse. |
| What I want may be delayed: recovering from an illness; the success of a project; an improvement in my relationships. But I'm sure the best is yet to come. | Life doesn't bode well for me. I won't recover from my illness, my project won't succeed and my relationships with others as well as the way they treat me, will remain bad. |
| I may feel sad, upset, stressed or afraid, but these are normal, temporary human feelings. They're a part of life, but they will go away and things will get better. | I always feel sad and upset, I can't control my fear and all I get out of life is sorrow and misery. |
| This failure happened for a reason. I didn't want it to happen but I have to learn from it, as it was meant to be. | I failed because I'm a loser and I will never accomplish anything worthwhile, because circumstances are always against me! |

As we have already seen, the external circumstances that you face only influence ten per cent of your happiness. Your reactions have the biggest part in shaping your life; even more, they are the true foundation for your success, happiness and strength of character.

One researcher conducted a study on people who had a heart attack, to discover their reactions and perspective after the event. Some were pessimistic, considering the attack as a disaster and the end of the world. The attack as well as all their other problems filled their mind.

Others, however, were more optimistic. Their optimism doesn't mean that they were happy to have a heart attack; no one ever is. But they said, "I wish it didn't happen, but since it did, it must have an upside. For one, at least I'm still alive! I will consider this attack as an 'alarm bell' waking me up from my negligence and my lack of interest in my health and eating habits. It's also an 'alarm bell' to strengthen my ties with my family, who I neglected. Moreover, it's an 'alarm bell' to set my priorities in life and focus on the important things, rather than worry about banalities." This is the way to look for the positive, and this is how successful, happy people think.

Year later, the people who looked for the upside had lived longer, healthier and more stable lives than those who sought the negative. Furthermore, the possibility of them having another attack was less than the others.

***The optimist knows that, even if he doesn't face the best circumstances, he will still look for the best in the circumstances he goes through.***

This doesn't mean that the positivity seeker doesn't feel hurt, frustrated, angry, offended, or afraid. The main difference between the optimist and the pessimist is that the former knows that, even if he doesn't face the best circumstances, he will still look for the best in the circumstances he goes through. He is also very hopeful that things will get better. This is how the positivity seeker thinks. In other words, every problem is temporary and meant to be, and you will get rewards and benefits out of it. So, look for the bright side and you will notice positive changes in your life, your happiness and your peace of mind. "It may be that you hate something in which God has set much good."

Remember, the problems and difficulties we encounter can improve, teach and strengthen us. That is why a wise man called them "opportunities for development". The friend who bothers you and raises your blood pressure may be a godsend to learn patience and endurance. Likewise, falling ill can be an 'alarm bell' that teaches you to mind your health, and draw your attention to things you overlooked. As

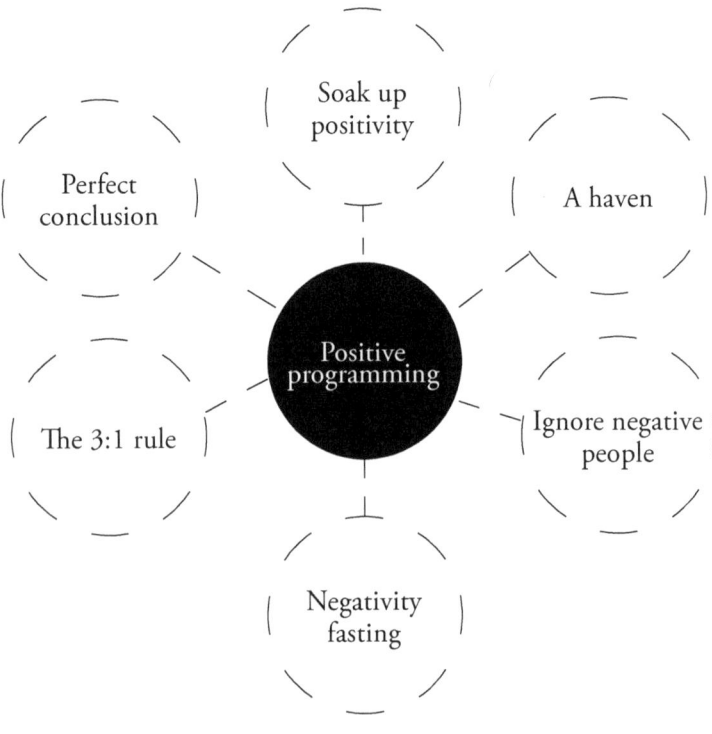

## THE POSITIVITY SEEKER AND THE NEGATIVITY SEEKER

for your failures, they might be a gift from God to teach you persistence and perseverance. Every event is an important moment in your life, and you have a choice: either you look for the positive, so you grow and rise up, or you look for the negative and keep being angry, grumpy and sad.

He said: Nights have forced me to swallow bitter gall.
I said: Smile, even if you were given bitter gall in strong doses.
Perhaps if someone saw you in good spirits.
He will discard gloom and rejoice instead.
Will complaining ever earn you a penny?
Will cheerfulness cost you anything?
There is no danger, Friend, in parting your lips.
Your face will not be disfigured if you smile.
Laugh, for the stars laugh when night is darkest.
It is for this reason we love the stars.
He said: Cheerfulness makes no one happy,
People come into this world and leave against their will.
I said: Smile, as long as an inch.
Separates you from death; for once dead, you will smile no more.

# Lean Towards Positivity

But how do I get myself to think positively? This is an important, often asked question. Here, we will discuss six ways that help positive programming.

As we can see in the figure, there are six methods that can help us with positive programming.

**1. Soak up positivity:** what is meant by this and how can your mind soak up positivity? If you receive a blessing or go through a positive situation, don't ignore it. Remember it, replay it in your mind and thank God for it. Don't let it pass you by without feeling gratitude and joy, which help your mind be more positive. Not even if it's something that is – in your opinion – small, like finishing a task, sitting with your family or friends, waking up healthy. In so doing, you fill your mind with positive, encouraging, tolerant, loving, self-justifying, self-boosting, comforting thoughts. The point is to help our mind soak up positivity, because a negative situation is stored in the mind three times faster than a positive one, which quickly disappears if we don't acknowledge it.

*You create a safe haven by focusing on the greater blessings in your life.*

**2.     A haven:** this is an important way to maintain positivity. As the author of The Happiness Project recommends: create a haven in your mind.

Having a safe haven in your mind is very important, because it helps you stay positive when going through a negative situation or when assaulted by pessimistic, dark thoughts. You create a haven by focusing on the greater blessings in your life. You can also have affirmations and pieces of wisdom that you memorized. For example, if you're in a bad situation, like someone driving recklessly or a friend upsetting you, remember more important things in your life, which are good: your family, your job, your children, your health, your studies, your future. Then you'll feel relieved, because you'll realise that your current situation is "nothing" compared to the greater blessings in your life. What's more, the people upsetting you aren't worth losing your happiness over.

**3.     Ignore negative people:** an important method of positively programming your mind is knowing how to ignore negative people, their suggestions and their thoughts. There are many ways to do this, such as transmitting some positivity to them. If you care about such a person, why not give him some good news to chase away his negative thoughts? For instance, if you're around someone who's pessimistic about the future or his finances, push him towards positivity by saying, "And in the heaven is your provision." Indeed, it is God who provides, not humans. And if you're with someone who's pessimistic due to fear or illness, push him to be positive by saying, "Be mindful and God will protect you." It is God who protects.

***You are a diverse mix of the characteristics of the five people you spend most your time with.***

Furthermore, don't pay too much attention to their words that might ruin your mood and try not to take them to heart. Even if you listen to them, don't give these words too much thought! Let them go in one ear and out the other.

Remember that you are a diverse mix of the characteristics of the five people you spend most your time with. Hence, if you spend your time with negative people, eventually, you will start resembling them; unless you counter their negativity with positivity and limit negative talk with them.

**4.     Negativity fasting:** As the body needs a diet without unhealthy food, so does the mind. This would fortify it, cleanse it of toxins and programme it positively, leaving no room for negativity. One method of positive programming is to "fast", eliminating bad newscasts as well as websites that post about crime, violence, problems and diseases. What good is it to read news about a lost baby in China, or a murder in Cambodia, or family problems in another city?

Unfortunately, the media, social networks and WhatsApp are full of bad news. If you make a habit out of reading bad news, you would be programming your mind negatively! Did you know that the ratio of negative news in the media and online networks reaches up to 17:1 bad news to good? This is guaranteed to programme you negatively.

Focus on websites that benefit your life and health; that educate and entertain you. Learn how to skip negative subjects and news.

LEAN TOWARDS POSITIVITY

**5.     The 3:1 rule:** the 3:1 rule is a way to positively programme your relationships. This means that, for example, when you criticize something a friend posted on social media or something you child or your wife did or when you wrong someone, you should stop your criticism and send three positive, encouraging and supportive messages, so that your positive attitudes are three times greater than the negative ones. No need to point out the positive in that situation; the idea is to halt criticism and not empty your relationship with others of positivity. Let optimism, praise and appreciation of others be the fixture, and criticism an occasional, temporary occurrence. For the Prophet (may peace be upon him) never expressed disapproval of food, nor did he ever criticise Anas, even though he served him for ten years! This is the proper way to treat others.

This rule doesn't just apply to your reactions. Even when you think of a negative situation involving your friend or spouse, immediately think of three positive ones instead. This method will make you more disciplined, reducing your anger and emotional reactions and increasing your emotional intelligence.

Don't think that you would become weak if you were more positive towards others. On the contrary, you would grow stronger because you would be disciplined in your feelings and balanced in your reactions. In so doing, you would energize yourself as well as others. Indeed, in an experiment conducted by scientist Goddard to measure energy levels, it was shown that energy increases when hearing a word of encouragement and decreases in the face of criticism. Remember, a kind word is charitable.

***End your day thinking of three positive things that happened to you that day or that week, without leaving out the simple and joyful things.***

6. **The perfect conclusion:** another method of positive programming is to end your day on a positive note, as recommended by the author of This Year I Will… Our religion has always urged us to do so, since the Morning and Evening Remembrances are a positive and encouraging end to the day. In a nutshell, this method consists of adopting a new bedtime ritual at least once a week – every Friday, for instance. That evening, think of three positive things that happened to you that day or that week. If big events occurred, then remember them, but without leaving out the simple and joyful things, such as doing a good job, spending time with a friend, visiting your parents, having a nice meal, your child getting a good grade on a test, giving to charity, easing someone's distress, a wish coming true. Counting blessings and remembering them makes you feel good and fills your mind throughout the night. And you will wake up feeling the same way you did when you went to bed!

**WHAT SHOULD I DO?**
- Every day, pick a quiet time, and spend five minutes clearing your mind of negative thoughts. Have faith that today will be better than yesterday and that tomorrow will be better than today, as this is bound to soothe you.
- Be aware of your own thoughts.
- Are you focusing on the negative? Does your mind

lean towards negative thoughts? Does it look for flaws?
- ☞ Ignore all of these and stop making negative judgements that consume your energy and your happiness. Look for the positive aspects and the benefits of anything that happens to you during the day.
- ☞ Recall the six ways to positively programme the mind and apply them throughout the day.

**Scientific study:**
The study "Finding Positive Meaning in a Stressful Event and Coping," conducted by Suzanne C Thompson on people whose homes were damaged or destroyed by a fire.

**WHAT SHOULD I READ?**
*The Success Factor*, by John Leach.
*51 Ideas to Change Yourself and the World Around You*, by Béatrice Millêtre (written in Arabic).

# Minds Are Like Computers

When you feel guilty about something you did, remind yourself that you're human. You made a mistake, and you'll make others. This human trait is inescapable! Let yourself feel regret for a moment, then resolve to change for the better.

Our minds are like computers: they work the way we programme them to. You may own the best, most expensive computer, but if you misprogramme it, it can become the slowest, worst computer! This is one reason why many people lead miserable lives. Indeed, the main reason isn't their lack of means, talent or blessings, but the fact that they programmed their mind incorrectly. As a result, they're always criticizing and being hard on themselves, as if to punish themselves. If they make a mistake, they blame themselves for their luck, for not putting in more effort. They keep repeating self-denigrating statements, such as:

"I have always been unlucky. I can't make my hopes and dreams come true. My life is full of difficulties and distress. I have made so many mistakes…"

*Like a virus destroys the best, most expensive computer, negative thinking destroys your personality, your life and your happiness.*

Just like a virus destroys the best, most expensive computer, this way of thinking destroys your personality, your life and your happiness. If this is the way you think, you are bringing worry, fear and anger on yourself, which will neither benefit nor improve you.

***Excessive severity destroys your comfort and causes tension and anxiety.***

There are two ways to deal with our mistakes and flaws. The first one is self-flagellation and punishment, and the second is self-compassion.

- Self-flagellation and focusing on your flaws make the mind tense, distressed and fearful. Whereas self-compassion brings comfort and happiness
- Self-compassion is to be kind and forgiving towards yourself whenever you make mistakes, or face problems and difficulties
- Self-compassion means understanding the human condition: You're an imperfect human being who makes mistakes, just like everyone else
- Self-compassion is accepting yourself the way you are, with your qualities and your flaws, as well as accepting your mistakes without making a big deal out of them
- Self-compassion doesn't mean you won't feel sad when a problem occurs, or that you won't blame yourself when you're at fault. Rather, it means that you won't overdo these things

Sometimes, we believe we must lead a strict life, criticizing, berating ourselves and being firm, so that we become practical and achieve our goals, instead of slacking off or failing. But this severity that we expect to motivate us and push us forward, ends up destroying our peace of mind, our happiness and our positive feelings. Eventually, it could even make us stressed and afraid.

Instead of harshly criticizing yourself when you make a mistake or fail, forgive yourself and remember that you sometimes need failure to learn. It has been proven that people who don't berate themselves when they fail, and don't exaggerate their mistakes, are happier, more optimistic and more successful.

Suppose a dear friend comes to you, complaining about not getting a job, or not getting into college; how would you react? Would you tell him that he's a loser who brought this on himself for not applying himself in high school, and that he has no hope of succeeding? Or would you comfort and reassure him, telling him that the future is in God's hands?

You would do the latter, of course. But why? Because compassion towards others is in our nature, while self-compassion is hard for some. Studies have shown that self-compassion not only increases your happiness and optimism but also improves your relationship with others. Someone who's incapable of self-compassion won't be kind and forgiving with others because you can't give something you don't have! Hence, be as kind to yourself as you would be to your best friend and, God willing, your life will change for the better.

# The Present Moment Is the Key to Happiness

The present moment is all we have. Our peace of mind and clarity depend on our capacity to focus on the moment we're living. So don't let past problems and fear of the future rob you of your present.

A girl once asked her mother, "Dear Mum, what is the happiest moment on your life?"

The mother answered, "This is the happiest moment of my life!"

The girl was stunned and thought her mother had memory problems, or was mistaken. So, she said, "But what about your wedding night, or the beautiful moments we lived during last year's trip?"

Her wise mother replied, "True, these moments were the happiest of my life at the time. And now, sitting here with you, your dad and your siblings is the happiest moment of my life."

***You can't live happily if you're not living in the present.***

These wise words the mother said are one of the most important rules of happiness, which is to live in the moment. Ponder these words, my friend. You can't live happily if you're not living in the present and you won't feel the positive feelings that nourish happiness. You won't be cheerful during joyful times, nor will you be thankful when you receive blessings, nor enjoy your loved ones' affection at the appropriate time, nor be amazed by what you see. You will lose all these feelings because your mind will be stuck either in a past that's long gone, or in an unforeseeable future that isn't guaranteed!

***If you put off the chance to live life "now",
you might miss out on it and lose it completely.
"Now" is the time to start living.***

We ruin the beauty of life by overthinking the past or future. Indeed, happiness is living the in present moment; it's in everything we do. If you put off the chance to live life "now", you might miss out on it and lose it completely. "Now" is the time to start living.

A woman said wonderful words about living in the moment, comparing it to a train ride.

"We board this train at birth, wanting to cross the continent, because we believe there's a station there somewhere. We pass beautiful small countries, which we see through the window of the train of life: grain fields, fodder silos, mountains, valleys, level railway crossings, crowded buses alongside us. We pass cities and factories, but we don't notice or pay attention to them because we want to reach our destination. This station changes throughout our life. The stations vary depending on the stages of our lives, but for most people, they are leaving secondary school, graduating from university, a first promotion, then their children graduating from university, then retirement. Only when it's too late do we realize the truth: there are no stations! Cheerfulness lies in the journey itself; cheerfulness and happiness are the journey. Truth lies in these moments that we missed willingly along the way, because we were too eager to reach the station. Sooner or later, you will realize that there is no station and that life is about the journey. Read a book, have fun with your family and friends, mind your health and walk more, hug a baby, enjoy your favourite pastime. Don't carry the weight of the world on your shoulders, and laugh more. And on your journey, look for a way to make this world a more beautiful place."

***Not living in the moment isn't innate, it's something we acquire along the way.***

Many of us excel at worrying; we worry about many things at once; we let past problems, upsetting situations and hurtful words settle inside us! Sometimes, we jump to the future and start worrying about our financial situation, our future, our children's education, our work troubles. In a matter of minutes, we end up worried, upset and crushed! Not living in the present causes fear and worry, which is why some schools of thought in psychology treat the "fear of the present moment". Oddly, not living in the moment isn't innate: it's something we acquired along the way. Indeed, if you observe children, you will see them completely immersed in the moment they're living, as if they have neither past nor future. Hence, they enjoy what they're doing presently, whether they're playing, watching cartoons or whatever else they're doing. This is something many of us lose during their life. You need to accept your past, forget your future and surrender to the present moment. Yesterday has come and gone; tomorrow is a mystery known only to God. The present, however, is a gift that we hold in our hands right now. Living in the present moment means being happy, letting go of the past and not waiting for the future. It means being aware that every moment you're breathing is a blessing and a priceless gift from God.

If you want to lead a happy life, respect the present moment, focus on it with all your senses and completely enjoy what you're currently doing. When you're eating your breakfast, instead of flipping through your phone or thinking about what your friend told you last night or about what will happen tomorrow, focus on what's going on in that instant. Savour your delicious breakfast, enjoy the birdsong and the beautiful sky, and sense God's gifts – food, health and shelter. Not only will living in the moment make you happier, it will also increase your concentration, because multitasking is very distracting. Respect the present moment and you will become less distracted and anxious. Furthermore, your happiness will increase, your communication skills will improve and you will become calmer. Resist your desire for time-travel, live the present moment and be in control.

## The Inner Mirror

An emaciated boy was sitting in a deserted corner of the subway. He was distractedly begging and selling pencils at the same time. A businessman passed him by, dropping a dollar in his bag before hurriedly hopping on the subway. After a moment's thought, he got out, walked up to the boy, grabbed a few pencils and explained apologetically that he had forgotten to take the pencils he intended to buy.

He went on, "You're a businessman, just like me, and you're selling your merchandise at a very reasonable price." Then he took the next train.

At a social gathering years later, an elegant young man approached the businessman and introduced himself, "You probably don't remember me, and I don't even know your name, but I will never forget you for as long as I live!

You're the man who gave me back my self-respect and appreciation. I used to think that I was a beggar selling pencils, until you came along and told me I was a businessman!"

***Everyone has the seeds of happiness within them. All they have to do is water and nurture these seeds.***

What keeps a lot of people from being happy and successful? Everyone has the seeds of happiness within them. All they have to do is water and nurture these seeds for them to grow and thrive. But what can hinder the growth of these seeds, preventing people from being happy? If reality and studies are any indication, one of the greatest blocks is low self-esteem. It's the inner mirror: because our self-esteem and respect reflect our self-perception. We behave the same way we see ourselves, so change starts from within.

Many don't see themselves in a positive light, nor appreciate themselves, nor acknowledge the means that God has given them. They're convinced that they'll never be happy, that they don't deserve happiness or other people's acceptance and will never achieve success. This proves that a person's self-love, self-esteem and appreciation for his God-given abilities are an important pillar of happiness.

One successful man said about his experience: "I used to have bad self-perception, so whenever I would go into a meeting, or into a packed room in a public place, I would get negative thoughts and feelings like: 'What do they think of me? Why did I come here? You're inferior to the people attending this meeting, you won't bring anything to it!' and similar thoughts that clearly show my poor self-esteem."

***If you keep telling yourself that you deserve happiness, success and good things, your chances of getting what you want will increase.***

A lot of us have poor self-esteem; and it's not related to money, rank or beauty. Money, rank and beauty are pointless if you don't value yourself 100%. Many people have low-income jobs and aren't good looking or charismatic, but still love themselves, have a lot of self-confidence and lead a happy life. If you keep telling yourself that you deserve happiness, success and good things, your chances of getting what you want will increase, regardless of your reality. Conversely, if you criticize and put yourself down, and think you're unworthy or inferior to others, you will lose your motivation and drive, and happiness will be out of your reach, regardless of your fortune, beauty or rank.

Self-esteem is two-fold:

➤ • Believing that you can build a new life, as well as deal with circumstances and challenges that you will face along the way. Yes, you might go through challenges and circumstances, with your family, in your relationships, at work, or in your personal life. But God willing, you will be capable of dealing with them, giving it your best.

➤ • Believing in your worth as a human being, loving and appreciating yourself, having positive self-perception and not putting yourself down in front of others, or yourself.

Having self-esteem doesn't mean seeing yourself as the best and brightest person in the world. It simply means loving yourself for who you are. Having self-esteem doesn't mean not doubting your abilities at times, but rather, facing these doubts and refuting them instead of giving in to them.

*Instead of criticizing and belittling yourself, learn to be your own number one motivator and biggest cheerleader.*

# The Self-Esteem Quartet

Low self-esteem isn't something we're born with that can't be changed. Rather, it's acquired throughout life. And the rule states: "Anything you can acquire, you can get rid of." There are four tried-and-true ways to increase your self-esteem.

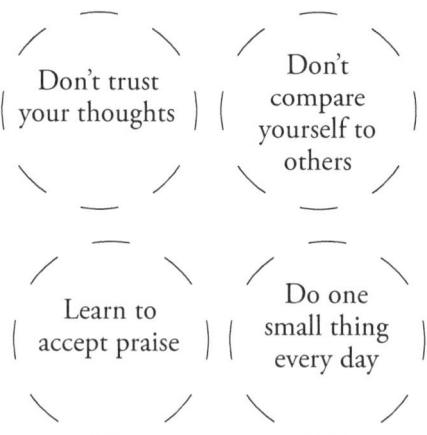

> **Don't trust your thoughts:** if you think about yourself in a negative, unappreciative way, you have first to stop trusting such discouraging thoughts that paint a distorted picture of you. These thoughts come from the subconscious, or negative programming during childhood, or from your friends, teachers,

the media, or your previous experiences. So, instead of criticising and belittling yourself, learn to be your own number one motivator and biggest cheerleader -- the president of your own fan club even! Every time you do a good job, don't let it go unnoticed, praise yourself. Every time you commit to self-imposed rules, don't think you did it out of duty, rather consider it as taking positive, helpful action. And every time you make a mistake, go easy on yourself, as if you were dealing with a child who should be taught gently. Instead of criticizing yourself, consider this mistake a step you can learn from.

***Whatever you own, there will always be someone who owns more. So don't compare yourself to others.***

***Compare yourself to what you want to be, and focus on what truly matters to you.***

➤ **Don't compare yourself to others:** when you go down the rocky road of social comparison, you always end up being the loser and the miserable one in any comparison. The reason for this is simple: we often compare ourselves to those who are better than us; and rarely to a homeless, poor or sick person. Comparing ourselves to richer, prettier, happier people has no end, and we can never come out on top. Indeed, whatever you own, there will always be someone who owns more. If you own a house, you will start looking for someone who owns one with a backyard; and if you own a house with a backyard, you will look for someone who owns a house with a playground. Even more depressing are those who compare themselves to celebrities, models, actors and athletes. Hence, the solution to self-esteem problems is "positive comparison", which is to compare yourself to what you want to be and focus on what truly matters to you. Just ignore other people's opinion of you, because our goal in life isn't to race others, but rather to prove ourselves, set up our own race and chase after whatever God intended for us. This is where happiness lies. And if you must resort to comparison, do as the Prophet (may peace be upon him) recommended: "Look at those who are lower than you (financially) but do not look at those who are higher than you, lest you belittle the favours God conferred upon you."

- **Learn to accept praise:** when a person feels bad about himself, naturally he will tend to reject any words of praise from others, thinking they're just being polite, or lying, because his inner mirror says otherwise. Hence, it's important you learn to accept praise, and feel comfortable doing so. Then, you respond with two magical words: "Thank you." If you do this, the outside world will strengthen your inner world and your inner mirror will change over time. For your part, don't forget to praise others. If you notice someone with beautiful hair or clothes, someone who smells good or does a good job – even writes a nice tweet – tell him so and praise him. This will make him feel good about himself and will increase your self-esteem and your happiness

➤ **Do one small thing every day:** having goals is one of the most important self-esteem boosters, since goals give your life meaning. Simply setting goals and not working towards them is, however, a negative, depressing thing. Nothing can be accomplished without work, and lack of activity is a big source of human frustration. Thus, make a habit of getting closer to your goals, even by one centimetre a day. Your life is full of goals, so thinking about them all at once might confuse you, since there's your health, your career, your family, your social life, your spiritual life. Which is why you should think: "What can I accomplish in each of these areas every day?" Don't get confused or worried, just start, even with something small; make it a daily habit, and you'll notice how it increases your self-esteem. Beware of exaggerated or idealistic goals and expectation, and remember: "Those which are done most continuously, even if they amount to little."

# Cut the Imaginary Ropes

A farmer went to his neighbour asking him for a rope with which to tie his donkey in the yard. The neighbour said he didn't have one and gave him this advice instead: "You can simulate the same movement around the donkey's neck. Pretend that you're tying it, and it won't run away!"

The farmer followed his neighbour's advice. The next morning, the donkey was still in the exact same spot. Wanting to go to the field, he gave the donkey a pat to get it to move, but it refused to! The man tried with all his might to get the donkey to move, to no avail. So, the farmer gave up and went once more to his neighbour for advice. The latter asked, "Did you pretend to loosen the donkey's rope?" The farmer answered in surprise, "There is no rope!" To which the neighbour replied, "To you there isn't. But to the donkey, the rope is there!" The farmer went home and pretended to untie the rope. And the donkey immediately followed its master without resistance!

Don't mock that donkey. People can also be prisoners of imaginary habits or beliefs that restrict their movement and limit their happiness. All they need to do is discover the invisible rope around their mind, which is stopping them from moving forward! This is exactly what happens to a lot of us. Say someone went through hard circumstances, problems, situations or bad experiences in the past. Consequently, he learned bad things about himself, like: "I have low self-confidence. I have a weak personality. My life can't get better. I have no hope of solving my problems." These wrong beliefs took hold of his mind, so he learned to become helpless and a quitter. Ever since then, he was led by the imaginary ropes he had placed around his neck.

In reality, learned helplessness and weakness is a common thing, as confirmed by scientific experiments. For example:
- Someone who is repeatedly insulted or assaulted without standing up for himself, puts an imaginary rope around his neck, learning weakness and cowardice in the face of those who robbed him of his rights
- When a father constantly reprimands his child, calling him "stupid", he puts an imaginary rope around his neck. The child then becomes convinced that he's stupid!
- If a person who tried once or twice to accomplish something and failed tells himself that he always will, and that he will never achieve what he wants, then he will learn defeat. He will lose his ambition, and put this imaginary rope around his mind and his life
- When children live a life of luxury, doing nothing, not having any tasks or responsibilities, they learn helplessness, thus losing self-confidence

Learned helplessness is just an imaginary rope created by a person's beliefs and delusions. Still, it's dangerous, as it can completely paralyze us and degrade our self-perception. If you visit a circus in India, you will be amazed to see a huge elephant secured with thin ropes that a child could cut! Is it magic or a supernatural force that keeps the giant elephant from cutting them? The answer is simple: when he was a baby, trainers used to tie the elephant with metal chains, so he would try to free himself at first. But after a few days, the poor baby elephant would stop trying due to pain and bruising. Once an adult, even though he becomes big and strong, weighing almost six tons, the 10-foot-tall elephant still thinks like a baby. So, he never tries to cut the thin ropes because he thinks: "It can't! It will hurt. I will never solve my problems. I will never succeed." His foot may be tied with a small, soft rope, but the real ties are his helplessness and his belief that he can't break loose no matter how much he tries! It's not his reality or a lack of strength that are stopping him, but his beliefs. The same goes for a lot of people. We all have the energy and strength to achieve what we want, but there are chains, ropes and beliefs stopping us. These beliefs keep us chained because of a childhood experience, another person's negative influence, a project, or a boss…

***When something bad happens, pessimists attribute it to their own weaknesses and failures.***

There are two ways of interpreting events and circumstances:
➤ The pessimistic, helpless way: When something bad happens, pessimists attribute it to their own weaknesses and failures. They think: "I'm not talented. It's my fault. My boss criticised me because I'm unqualified. I'm the problem. The boss reprimanded me, so I'm incompetent…" They always see themselves as the root of their problems. Of course, taking responsibility can sometimes be beneficial. But always blaming oneself

is destructive. Even if he succeeds, a pessimist rarely takes credit for it. For instance, if he gets promoted, he considers it a stroke of luck that won't happen again, or gives all the credit to his manager!

***An optimist avoids constant self-blame. He's fair, so he gives credit to God first, then to others, including himself.***

> In contrast, an optimist avoids constant self-blame. He's fair, so he gives credit to God first, then to others, including himself. To him, a bad situation is limited to a place or a person: "My colleagues dislike me… but not everyone else. I failed the maths course, but not the other subjects. The e-learning course I attended wasn't useful, but other courses were." The optimist might feel distressed in such a situation, but he carries on with his life with determination and persistence. The optimist also considers his failure a temporary event that will soon pass. Optimists view the future as "the next opportunity", and when a door closes, armed with their faith in God, they look for other doors elsewhere. Make optimism your motto. Always have the optimistic belief that the best outcome will happen and that you will achieve the best, for your faith in God will only bring you good things. And remember that we all have the strength of an elephant, so don't let a thin rope, a weak chain, an idea, a belief, a failed project, or something someone said hold you hostage! Cut every rope, break every chain, learn from every try, and awaken your God-given strength.

# WITH OTHERS

65. The Boy Who Profited from His Father's Actions
66. You're Helping Yourself
67. From $27 to $100,000
68. The Last Ride of the Night
69. Giving and Taking
70. Half a Medal Is Better Than No Medal
71. The Quintet of Great Relationships

# The Boy Who Profited from His Father's Actions

When you help others, not only does it improve their life, but it raises your self-esteem as well. Thus, you feel contentment and self-respect, and everything starts moving within you. You're helping yourself.

**That's what happened**
Omar was a little boy from a middle-class family, who worked hard alongside his dad at the cafe they owned. One day, a tired-looking traveller came in and ordered something to eat. Then Omar's dad noticed that the client looked like a dignified man of faith, so he said, "Go to the mosque nearby and rest. My son will deliver your order to you."

Once the man left for the mosque, Abu Omar made him a proper meal with the best ingredients at hand, then sent it along with his little boy. The stranger was in awe of Abu Omar's generous meal, so after he finished eating, he went to Omar's dad to thank him, saying, "You have been good to me, and I have nothing on me to pay you back. But I can tutor your son Omar, and share with him everything I memorized and learned."

Omar's father rejoiced at the news. Soon enough, the traveller, Abu Massud, started tutoring Omar, and noticed the boy's virtuosity and extraordinary intelligence. So, he took him to the great scholars of his time, which opened a lot of doors for Omar bin Abdul Karim Al-Rawasi.

His reputation started spreading, until he became one of the great scholars of Islam and a mentor to the likes of Al-Ghazali, Al-Baghdadi, Al-Jurjani and others.

Helping others benefits both parties. It's scientifically proven that offering help releases endorphins, which increase happiness levels and fight depression. Helping others is a way of helping yourself. What goes around, comes around; it benefits your happiness, your health, your children, your professional success, your future, in addition to the rewards that will be bestowed upon you. That little boy could have kept working with his dad at their small diner. The secret lies in your generosity and kindness towards others, without knowing the impact it will have on you, your family, your health and your children.

# You're Helping Yourself

One of the fastest ways to be happier, more mature and more loved is to lend a helping hand, to comfort, to treat others with dignity and generosity. That's why it's important to look for opportunities to help everywhere we go. This help isn't necessarily in the form of money, or a big gesture, as there are countless types of giving:
- Giving money
- Giving time
- Giving knowledge
- Giving compassion
- Giving love
- Granting forgiveness
- Giving the benefit of the doubt
- Praying for others is a form of giving
- Doing no harm is also a way of giving

Giving is to allow passage to a hurried driver, to send a letter of congratulations to someone on a special occasion, to comfort someone, to give a desperate person hope, to pay an electricity bill, to visit the sick, to guide a person, to smile at others. It's to be skilled and sincere, whether you're a father, a teacher, an engineer or a doctor. Any charitable action will increase your happiness level. Indeed, a study has showed that those who do five kind acts – however little – are five times happier than indifferent people. If you want to increase your happiness level, keep asking yourself, "What can I offer?" instead of "What can I gain?", for giving in the name of God grants you happiness and peace of mind. Whereas if you "give" only to "get" in return, you will feel cheated and will be deprived of serenity, feeling angry instead! Giving for the sake of it is rewarding and makes you feel better. As the saying goes, "If you want to be happy for an hour, take a nap. If you want to be happy for a day, go fishing. If you want happiness for a month, get married, and if you want happiness for a year, get rich. But if you want a lifetime of happiness, help others."

In addition to improving your life and happiness, helping others is one of the most valued deeds in the eyes of God. Meditate on this great Hadith, in which helping others is considered better than an entire month's retreat in the Prophet's Mosque.

The most beloved of people to God is the one who brings most benefit to people, and the most beloved of deeds to God is making a Muslim happy, or relieving him of hardship, or paying off his debt, or warding off hunger from him. For me to go with my Muslim brother to meet his need is dearer to me than observing a retreat in this mosque for a month. Whoever goes with his Muslim brother to meet his need, God will make him stand firm on the Day when all feet will slip. And wickedness and evil behaviour destroy and spoil good deeds just as vinegar spoils honey.

***When we stop giving and caring about others, we reduce our happiness, because happiness is a feeling that spreads from one person to another.***

In a study conducted at a college, called "The Connection Between Spending & Happiness", a group of students were given cash and told to spend it on themselves, buying whatever clothes, food or accessories they needed. Their happiness level was monitored during the experiment, and it was concluded that shopping increases happiness for a limited amount of time – a week at most.

Then, another group of students was given the same amount of cash and asked to spend it on needy people: a beggar, a street sweeper, a homeless person, a relation in need. After the experiment, their happiness level was measured, and it was revealed that their happiness lasted for a whole month. Who says taking makes you happy? Even if the opposite seems true, giving is sweeter than receiving. The pleasure of taking is shared by most of mankind, but the pleasure of giving is known only to the great, and people of high morals.

When we stop giving and caring about others, we reduce our happiness, because happiness is a feeling that spreads from one person to another. So, if you want to be forgiven, forgive. If you want to be spared, spare others. If you want to be helped, offer help. And if you want to be happy, make other people happy. Give what you would like to receive, and it will always come back around. When you help others attain happiness, you are overcome with relief and satisfaction.

***Never regret giving. You may give to some and be met with ingratitude.***

Actions speak louder than words. You can constantly say sweet and wonderful things to others, but what you give them solidifies your words. Don't wait for special occasions or holidays to give. On an ordinary day, without cause for celebration, give something beautiful, say surprising words or write a letter of thanks to your spouse, your siblings, your children, your co-worker, a stranger. You'll be amazed at the happiness that will surround you all.

Never regret giving. You may give to some and be met with ingratitude, or be ignored. Hence, it's very important to consider giving a principle of yours, not a reaction! Never stop giving under the excuse that no one deserves it, because you may be right, and people might in fact be unworthy. But what about you? Don't you want to be worthy of God's rewards? On the first day of the Revelation, our Lady Khadija herself (may God be pleased with her) swore that God would not disgrace Muhammad (may peace be upon him); why? You keep good relations with your kith and kin, help the poor and the destitute, serve your guests generously and assist the deserving calamity-afflicted ones.

# From $27 to $100,000

A waitress handed a lunch menu to two ladies. Without looking at it, they asked her what the two cheapest meals were, since they didn't have enough money. Sarah, the waitress, didn't take long to answer, suggesting two meals. They immediately followed her meal recommendation, as long as it was the cheapest.

They ate the plates she brought over and once done, asked for the bill. Soon, Sarah came back with a paper inside a folder, where she had written: "Considering your situation, your bill was paid from my personal account. This is the least I could do. Thank you for your kindness. Signed: Sarah." The surprising thing about this incident is that Sarah felt an overwhelming joy after paying the bill, despite her difficult financial situation, since she was saving up to buy a TV. But what saddened her was her friend's reaction, reprimanding her and denouncing her behaviour. Then she got a phone call from her mum, screaming, "What did you do?"

Sarah answered, "I didn't do anything. What happened?!" Her mum replied, "You're getting praise on Facebook. Two ladies published the note you wrote them after paying their bill, and everybody is sharing it! I'm proud of you." Sarah immediately opened her Facebook account and found hundreds of messages from producers and reporters asking for an interview to talk about her incredible gesture.

The next day, Sarah appeared live on one of the most

famous TV programmes, which presented her with a new television and ten thousand dollars. Gifts kept pouring in and their value reached a hundred thousand dollars; all this in exchange for two meals that cost her no more than twenty-seven dollars! What she had was multiplied by her generosity. A single wheat ear sprouted seven others, each with a hundred grains!

***Helping others is like a traveller's bag on the luggage belt. It may disappear, but it's bound to come back to you.***

Anything you give away will surely come back to you sooner or later. The favour won't necessarily be returned by the same person and in the same way but you can be sure that you'll get something in exchange for what you give others – whether it's money, a rose, a smile, a visit, an act of charity, a gift. The only condition is to give in the name of God, without expecting anything in return, and He will compensate you for everything you spend. Indeed, helping others is like a traveller's bag on the luggage belt. It may disappear, but it's bound to come back to you.

When King Khosrow passed by an old sheikh who was planting an olive tree, he asked him, "You are so very old, what use is this plant to you? Do you think you will be alive long enough to eat its fruit?"

The sheikh answered, "All my life, I have been eating olives from trees that my grandfather planted. It's time to plant my own."

Khosrow was impressed with the old man's wisdom. Despite having a fortune, he was in awe, and exclaimed, "Wow."

The Sheikh said, "Do you see, O King, how quickly my plant has yielded fruit!"

Khosrow answered, "Wow!"

The Sheikh continued, "O King, this type of tree bears fruit once a year, but my tree bore fruit twice."

Khosrow said, "Wow," then left.

# The Last Ride of the Night

Once, a professor in medicine at a college in Alexandria surprised her students with a statement: "I will be giving you any book we use in this course for free."

Although the students appreciated her generosity they were perplexed, knowing how expensive medical books were. One student said, "Thank you, Doctor. But why?"

The doctor answered, "Listen to this: twenty-five years ago, a man by the name of Ahmad Abdel Tawab, who was in a precarious financial situation, wished for his daughter to get into medical school. So did she, and their wish came true when she got accepted.

One day, the university asked her to pay 350 Egyptian Pounds for books and other fees. The girl's father was a simple man who worked as a minibus driver, so it would be difficult for him to provide such an amount of money. When his daughter told him about the expenses, he didn't complain. Rather, he said, 'May God grant us good things.' On that rainy evening, he took the bus for a drive, hoping to find some clients and raise the money he needed.

Along the way, he picked up an elegant man. Ahmad recounts, 'I was surprised that the man was taking the bus, even though he looked rich. I asked him about it and he told me his car had been stolen. Later that evening, I came across a family that was soaking wet from the rain, so I picked them up, and told them, "The last ride of the night

## THE LAST RIDE OF THE NIGHT

is free." The family happily welcomed the news.

The rich man turned to me and asked, "Why?"

I told him that my family and I had agreed that the last ride of the night would be an offering to God, hence it would be free.

As the family was getting off the bus, I asked them to wish my daughter Fatima good luck in medical school.

Then the rich man asked me, "Who's Fatima?"

I told him that she was attending medical school and how the college had asked her for money to continue her studies. I had a picture of her in front of me, so the man asked, "This is your daughter?"

I answered, "Yes."

The man reached his destination and paid me 200 Egyptian Pounds, which I gave to my daughter. She was upset that it didn't cover all her fees and said, "I wish you had charged for the last ride."

I replied, "My daughter, blessed is what we gave to God".'

Fatima was in class when she got called over to the dean's office. Not knowing why he would want to see her, she went to his office, where he first asked her, 'Are you Fatima Ahmad Abdel Tawab?'

She answered, 'Yes, that's me!'

He said, 'From now on and until you graduate, come to me with anything you need and all your requests will be granted.'

All this because the last ride of the night was free. For what is done in God's name is never done in vain."

Then the professor said, "Now allow me to introduce myself: I am Fatima Ahmad Abdel Tawab."

***You can be certain that whatever seeds you plant in others, God will plant them in you in this lifetime. You get back what you gave to others when you need it.***

You can be certain that whatever seeds you plant in others, God will plant them in you in this lifetime. You get back what you gave to others when you need it. Moreover, giving is one of the most fulfilling pleasures of life. When you give, you charge yourself with a more positive, greater energy than what you gave away.

When we trust that what we offer today will come back to us sooner or later, we will be generous in acts and in manners. We will know that it will all come back around, and giving will become a source of pleasure and joy.

*Do not walk among people without having mercy for them and do not treat them except with fairness.*

*And cut off the strength of all the hatred you harbour, even if a tongue slipped or a mind erred.*

*And shield yourself from what is not righteous and cover people with righteousness and kindness.*

*And if someone does good by you, reward him for his deed many times over.*

*And do not expose the abuse of an abuser and strengthen the ties with your harsh, ingrate kin.*

# Giving and Taking

Giving is wonderful. Yet, you will find people whose heart only has room for taking without anything in return! They are "addicted" to taking, and if you were a sea, they would drink you whole and still be thirsty. Over time, such people will drain your power, your energy and your happiness, so it's important to watch out for experts in taking. Although giving is a good thing, you shouldn't let others take advantage of your generosity. Be careful about people who constantly take. Be honest with them, don't commit to more than you can handle, don't carry more than you can bear and don't be afraid to say "no". There are also people who love to give and spend on others but are incapable of taking, because they think it's wrong or selfish – which is completely untrue. When you accept a "gift" from someone, you make them happy and glad, which means that you're giving as well as receiving. Furthermore, when you accept and thank them for their gift it brings them happiness, which in turn increases your own.

***It is necessary to open ourselves up to the world and learn how to give as well as receive.***

There are those who love to keep taking and receiving but hate giving and always expect others to help them. In order to evolve and live comfortably, it's important to understand the cosmic laws and the balance of life. One of these important laws is that life is about "give and take". It is necessary to open ourselves up to the world, and learn how to give as well as receive.

### *Live according to the principle: "Shine forth your light like a lamp for yourself and others to see."*

Don't be a candle that burns itself to light up other people's lives. A candle burns and wastes away, and is quickly consumed. This will be your case if you give to the point of forgetting yourself and your needs. Live according to the principle: "Shine forth your light like a lamp for yourself and others to see." Thus, you would be starting with yourself first and doing what benefits you, instead of neglecting yourself and your goals. And at the same time, you would do good by others but without harming yourself. For instance, there are mothers who sacrifice themselves to raise their children! This hurts them in the long run, which benefits neither them nor their children. The Prophet himself forbade the person who wanted to give all his money to charity from doing so because he would be harming himself and those closest to him. Indeed, in the Hadith it is said: "None of you [truly] believes until he loves for his brother that which he loves for himself." This means that you should wish yourself well first before wishing it to others.

#### What should I do?
**The week of giving:**
Make this week the week of giving. Don't let a day pass by without intentionally giving something to others. Here are some ideas to consider:

- Sense the needs of your loved ones this week – your parents, your siblings, your family
- Smile at a stranger and thank him. Be it a store clerk or a waiter, make his day brighter
- Answer a question someone asked on a website or on social media
- Pray for others in their absence
- Visit a sick person or congratulate a friend who had a baby and get the baby a gift, even a symbolic one
- Give a cup of water, a hot or a cold drink to a construction worker or a street sweeper
- Help someone in need, give up your seat for someone, let a hurried customer pass you in line
- Empathize with someone who needs sympathy
- Lend a hand using your skills and your line of work
- Without waiting for an occasion, give a gift,or thanks, or a beautiful letter to a co-worker
- Tip the delivery guy, your mechanic, your plumber or your tailor
- Help a co-worker or a schoolmate
- Give your wife a hand at home: hire help for the day
- Remember, the more you help others, the more God will help you; for God is merciful towards the charitable

**Scientific study:**
"Helping Others, Helping Ourselves", 2006.

### What should I read?
*Good deeds: Thirty Gates to Goodness*, by Muhammad Mus'ad Yaqut (written in Arabic).

# Half a Medal Is Better Than no Medal

Best friends Sueo and Nishida, who were both pole vault jumpers, got selected to represent Japan at the Berlin Olympics. After many rounds of competition the two athletes came face to face, competing for second place. The competition was so fierce that results were tied for hours straight; neither one of them could beat the other. Eventually, the referee decided to end the competition, calling a draw between the two athletes, which was a peculiar result, never seen before at the Olympics! The Olympics committee left it to the Japanese delegation to decide which one would get which medal. The delegation leaders deliberated and agreed to give the silver medal to Nishida, because he won the first jump, and the bronze to Sueo.

When the two friends returned to Japan, they had a wonderful idea. They took their medals to a jeweller who cut them both in half. Then he joined half of the silver medal with half of the bronze medal, creating a half-silver, half-bronze medal for each of them. The medals became known as "The Medals of Friendship".

***Friendship is one of the things that increase the happiness index the most.***

Friendship is one of the things that increase the happiness index the most. Friendships are a direct cause of many of our joys and sorrows. That's why we can't know real happiness without having real friends.

### *Even your successes are of little value if there is no one to share your joy with.*

A life without good friends who motivate us, who share our thoughts, feelings, success, failure, joy and sadness is a truly lonely one. Your real fortune is your friends. Moreover, the level of success you achieve in life and its reflection on your happiness are strongly related to the quality of your relationships. Even your successes are of little value if there is no one to share your joy with. As someone once said, "Joy and success are meaningless if you reach the top of a mountain alone." There's no such thing as a self-made person because everyone needs friendship and encouragement. As for those who try to do everything by themselves, they are bound to get into trouble. Even our Prophet Moses asked God to give him a minister and an assistant; so God Almighty sent Aaron to Moses to be his supporter and helper, and made Abu Bakr – who gave equal rights to the migrant and supporter tribes – his best friend. There is no happy tale in which friends, parents, spouses or loved ones don't play a part. Furthermore, the lack of good friendships is closely linked to anxiety, depression, addiction, low immunity, high stress and insomnia. Conversely, gravely ill people with strong friendships and a supportive family have higher recovery and survival rates than those with few friendships and supportive relationships.

# The Quintet of Great Relationships

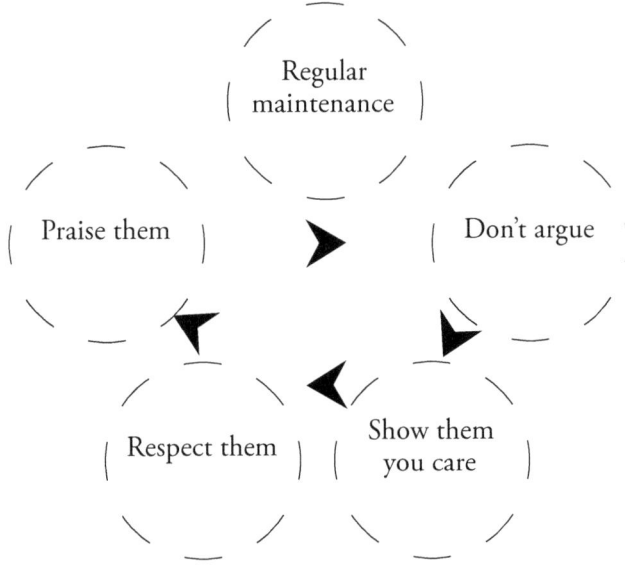

Maintaining great friendships and making new one are very important, essential for those who want to get ahead in life and increase their happiness index. Making friends isn't hard or complicated. Here are the five skills that will help you in your relationships:

• **Regular friendship maintenance:** just like equipment and cars need regular maintenance, so do our relationships, lest they break down. You maintain relationships through oral and written communication, which keeps them fresh and warm. To avoid neglecting your relationships, which would drastically increase their maintenance cost, you can divide them into three levels, depending on your closeness and the strength of your bond. Thus, level one would consist of your family and close ones, which require weekly maintenance. The next level needs monthly maintenance and the third, a semi-annual one. Note that live communication is essential while using this technique, because nothing can replace a face-to-face meeting. Indeed, as it has been said, "Seeing a loved one face to face for minutes raises your happiness level for a week."

***Every time you win an argument, you lose a friend, even if you're right!***

• **Don't argue:** arguments dampen relationships and weaken friendships; they're one thing you can't win! It's a lose-lose situation, because every time you win an argument, you lose a friend, even if you're right. Arguing doesn't amount to any good, especially when it's about subjects that have nothing to do with you, like politics or the economy. So, have constructive discussions by avoiding fruitless arguing. As for the topics where you have a say, your discussion of them should revolve around the idea, not the person. If you ever find yourself arguing with a friend, let your friendship rise above the situation and remember the words of our Prophet: "I guarantee a house in Paradise for one who gives up arguing, even if he is in the right."

• **Show them you care:** people generally like to feel valued. Showing interest in them and sharing their feelings, their burdens and their joys, captures their heart. It also increases your happiness and tips the balance of good deeds in your favour. If you're going through something and your friend sends you a message asking how you're doing and how he can help, it will have a big impact on you, making you feel strong and happy! And as we have seen, what goes around, comes around – it's a cosmic law. So show others that you care: if someone is sick, check up on them; if they're worried, comfort them; if they lose someone dear, share their grief; and if they're happy, share their happiness

• **Respect them:** other people's feelings can bring you closer or drive you apart. Respect is a mutual feeling: the more you respect and appreciate others, the more they return the feeling. Avoid hurting them, wounding them with your words, criticizing them or ignoring them in their presence. Furthermore, don't belittle them, make them feel bad about themselves or their situation, or badmouth them behind their back. To respect other people's feelings is not to gloat about things you have that they lack. Don't brag about your strength to someone weak, about your happiness to someone sad, about your freedom to a prisoner, or about your wealth to someone poor.

• **Praise them:** if you contemplate the life of the Prophet, you'll notice that he often praised his companions. Yet many of us find ourselves constantly thinking about other people's mistakes and flaws, which fills us with negativity towards them. Consequently, we find it hard to praise those closest to us: our spouse, our children, our friends. The next time you see a relation or friend, you won't need more than 30 seconds to break that barrier of negativity. Find a way to thank them for something they did for you or someone else, highlight one of their feats, or praise a quality of theirs. This will have a positive effect on them, as well as free you from negativity. Praise others out loud and criticize them privately because we raise ourselves up by lifting others. And as the saying goes: "Be and act like someone you would like to meet."

How do you praise others?
- ☛ Make sure the praise is truthful
- ☛ Be specific; mention the place and time, and what he said or did
- ☛ Say it as soon as possible
- ☛ Express your feelings

*Since I have known him, I have only been obedient to my friend. Blaming the brothers is not my concern.*

*My companion commits sins and I allow his sins, so that my forgiveness and kindness show.*

*If my friend does not persist in his misbehaviour, then what use are my forgiveness and kindness?*

*He wrongs me and I have mercy, always forgiving. There is nothing better than forgiving the guilty.*

# YOUR GOALS ARE YOUR FUTURE: NO GOALS, NO HAPPINESS

72. Break the Branch
73. Life Begins Outside the Comfort Zone
74. Circles of Life
75. Goals Are Happiness
76. The Law of Exponential Growth
77. Growth Mindset and Fixed Mindset
78. Don't Give Up

# Break the Branch

Living in the comfort zone makes you feel that you can't cross your limits. The comfort zone is a shell and a prison that prevents you from stepping out into the world of change.

**That's what happened**
A merchant from the Arabian Peninsula gave two beautiful young falcons to an Indian king. These falcons were of the best-known types of hunting birds, the Peregrine Falcon. The king was pleased with the gift and ordered a member of his court to train these falcons for hunting. Several months later, the trainer came to the king and informed him that he had succeeded in training one of the falcons for hunting but he had failed to train the other, who couldn't surpass its own branch. The king asked his assistants for advice but none of them knew the secret of the falcon's failure to learn. One of the king's aides suggested that the king seek the help of an Arab trainer, and indeed the king asked them to search for a falconry expert.

The falconry expert arrived and requested a week to train the falcon. He went to train the falcon and a week later, returned to inform the king that he had succeeded in teaching the falcon to hunt. Astonished, the king requested to see the falcon himself to ensure that it had learned to hunt. And that's what happened! The king saw the falcon soaring in the sky and catching its prey. He turned to the expert in amazement and asked him, "But how did you teach it?" The expert replied, "The secret is very simple; I broke the branch."

**Ask yourself:** what's the branch stopping you from achieving change and progress in life? What's the branch stopping you from achieving your goals/your happiness? We were all made to fly, soar, and be happy; and we were all born with big abilities and capabilities. When you step out of your comfort zone, you will discover new places, friends, hobbies, and feelings, as well as a potential you didn't know you had. The fear of experiencing new things and staying in your comfort zone are obstacles to happiness!

# Life Begins Outside the Comfort Zone

When was the last time you did something new? Read a book outside your field of specialty, for example? Visited a place for the first time? Took a different road to work? When was the last time you spoke with someone outside your circle of friends or family members? When was the last time you learned something new or broke a bad habit that was keeping you up at night? Many people have great difficulty doing new things that aren't part of their habitual daily routine, which they have been repeating over and over for years on end.

If in the past week you didn't do anything that challenges your abilities, teaches you something new, expands your skill set or changes a negative view of yours, then you didn't step out of your comfort zone. This means that your life is a never-ending routine. Coming out of the comfort zone is one of the most important causes of success and happiness.

We are all used to certain ideas and behaviours in our daily lives, to the point that if they change, even for the better, it might cause us tension. In turn, this has us running back to our "cocoon". We created this vicious circle ourselves: we programmed it and started refusing to get out of it.

*Fear stops a lot of people from experiencing new things, because they can't do or say something they're not used to.*

Fear (of criticism, of failure, of rejection, of bad results) stops a lot of people from experiencing new things because they can't do or say something they're not used to. Their mind was programmed with old thinking patterns, some of which are beneficial and some harmful. Yet they adapted to these patterns, even when it caused them misery, distress and weakness. Change became hard, scary and unnatural to them, because it meant entering the world of the unknown.

You need to accept the fear that accompanies stepping out of the comfort zone. Indeed, it's normal for something new to be scary at first, so don't let this fear control you. When we try to change anything – a job, our behaviour, an idea – it's bound to cause a little fear, which can be positive if it pushes you towards change. But if it makes you retreat and flee, then it's negative fear. Remember that the unknown can be frightening at first, but repetition makes it familiar. As ancient scholars used to say: "Neither the shy nor the arrogant can attain knowledge."

A rich man once came up to a swimming instructor in a well-known resort and said, "I'm so-and-so, owner of a famous shop, and I want you to teach me how to swim."

The coach replied, "Excellent. I will teach you to swim easily."

The rich man then looked around and saw a group of tourists, children and employees around the pool. So he said, "But I can't learn in front of all these people. Everybody would know that I'm learning to swim, and I don't look good in a swimsuit."

The teacher answered, "There's a condition you have to accept in order to learn how to swim, otherwise you never will."

The rich man asked, "What is it?"

The coach said, "To be able to take off your shirt, put on a swimsuit and show your belly to everyone."

Step onto the battlefield and don't be afraid of beginners' mistakes or the dread of change.

# Circles of Life

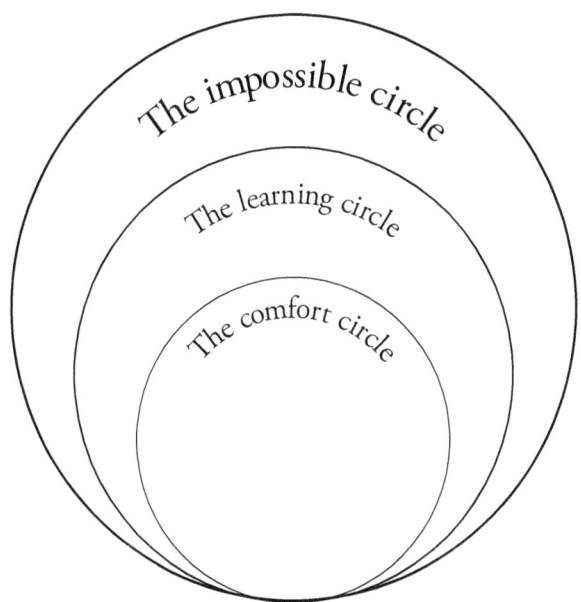

**The comfort circle**

It's the circle in which we live, where we feel safe, being comfortable within its limits. We don't like to leave or change it, even if it's wrong or limits our potential, our success and our happiness. For example:
➤ Staying in a specific friendship and not expanding, even though this friendship might be negative or frustrating

- Sitting for hours in front of the TV or your smart phone and not having a daily workout routine, or reading, or memorizing the Quran, or learning a foreign language, or doing something constructive
- Turning down a promotion just because it entails a location change
- We always feel comfortable and safe in our own comfort zone but, unfortunately, there isn't much room for growth and evolution in there. In addition, staying in that zone stops us from discovering abilities or skills that we never knew we had.

*Things won't happen on their own. If you want something, you have to "do" something about it.*

## The learning circle (expansion)

It's a bigger circle than the comfort one. It's where we start expanding our knowledge, our experience and our abilities, and strengthening our personality. How do you move to the learning circle? Start with small daily steps. The most important thing is to keep going. Move, do something, as others won't do it for you and things won't happen on their own. If you want something, you have to "do" something about it. Accomplishing and learning something – however small – every day brings you closer to a better tomorrow. When you improve yourself on a daily basis, you guarantee your progress towards the life you want and you keep learning; for a journey of a thousand miles begins with a single step.

Try something new regularly, so you get out of your comfort zone, and expand your learning zone. Visit unusual places, subscribe to an online English course, sit with new people, discuss an idea you're scared to talk about, move towards your goals, replace a bad habit with a healthy one. Don't reject something just for being new or unfamiliar. Be a student of life, hear and listen. I don't know what your goals are, or what you want to accomplish; but I'm sure that if you move every day – however slowly – towards your goal, you will achieve more than you can imagine.

**The impossible circle (pain)**
The impossible circle is the one who have to suffer to reach. It's the things we're afraid of, that we think will never happen, or that we could never do or achieve. For instance, some people believe they will never learn a foreign language, some think they could never speak in front of a crowd and others highly doubt they'll ever become a manager or a successful entrepreneur.

When you expand your comfort circle, move to the learning circle and improve yourself, your skills and your personality daily, you turn the learning circle into a comfort circle, and the impossible circle becomes a new learning circle. The fear is taken out of the learning circle, your beliefs change, which expands the impossible circle, turning it into a learning circle free from fear. Hence, all the circles change; such is the life of the successful.

At university, we had a beginners' English course. The student among us who knew the language the least happened to be bold. So, he got out of the comfort circle into the learning one, always asking questions without caring about the mistakes he made or the difficulty he had. The rest of us preferred to remain silent and not take any risks, thus remaining in our comfort zone. After a few months, the daring student became the best English speaker; his impossible circle had become a learning circle. He even set a new goal, and a new impossible circle: passing the TOEFL test. As for the rest of us, we stayed in the comfort circle for a long time, until we finally decided to get past our fear.

***Getting out of our comfort zone means doing things we've never done before.***

**How do I get out of the comfort zone?**
Leaving the comfort zone proves that we're still alive, that we still have dreams and ambitions to live for and strive to achieve, that we're still willing to sacrifice times of comfort and reassurance in pursuit of happier, more comfortable, safer, livelier, more satisfying and more self-fulfilling times.

Getting out of our comfort zone means doing things we've never done before, saying things we've never said, and thinking in a different way. You can be sure that the first step you take outside of your comfort zone won't be pleasant; for the first step in a journey of a thousand miles is the most difficult and stressful. You will feel the tension inside and you will encounter resistance that prevents you from continuing, feeling nostalgic for the comfort circle. But continuing to do the uncomfortable thing will eventually make it comfortable for you.

Start with easy things outside your circle (baby steps). For example, if you aspire to become an orator, don't go out in front of a crowd right away. Rather, practise on your own, then speak in front of a small group, and your self-confidence will improve (the learning circle). Gradually start expanding and you will get out of the learning circle into the impossible circle. You will expand your comfort circle; you will speak in front of people and gain confidence in yourself.

Similarly, if you want to lead a healthier, more active life, don't start with a strict workout regimen; don't torture yourself lifting heavy weights or walking for endless hours. Start with an easy programme that you can complete, pick people to help and encourage you, then gradually start improving and changing. Most people who join a gym quit after the first week because of their reaction to the sudden, brutal lifestyle change. "For the one who traverses it harshly will neither reach (his goal) nor will it spare anyone."

Likewise, if you want to venture into the world of reading, don't buy a handful of books in one day and don't read a dozen pages right away. Just try to do easy and simple things, which you know from personal experience you can successfully complete. Five pages are very sufficient in the beginning, since it doesn't matter how many pages you read! What matters is that you start. You shouldn't care too much about results at this stage but focus on the one sure thing: that you start breaking bad habits and acquiring new ones that elevate your life.

***You will face temptations and things that stand in the way of the change you seek, trying to pull you back into your cocoon.***

Remember that you will face temptations and things that stand in the way of the change you seek, trying to pull you back into your cocoon. Every time you find yourself retreating to your cocoon – for example, turning to social media, or getting distracted on your phone when you have work to finish, or reading or chores to do – don't succumb to distractions. Give yourself twenty minutes to complete your task, after which you can spend five minutes on social media before getting back to work.

Even in worship, moderation and a gradual approach are key. The Prophet himself (may peace be upon him) said to Abdullah bin Omar, "O Abdullah, have I not been informed that you fast all day, and stand in prayer all night?" He answered, "You have, O Prophet." So the Prophet said, "Don't do that. Observe fast and break it; sleep and get up for prayer, for your body has a right over you, your eyes have a right over you and your wife has a right over you. And observe fast for three days during the month; for every good is multiplied ten times and that will be equal to fasting the whole year."

Getting out of your comfort zone the right way enhances your creativity and increases your productivity. It brings you to unexpected stages of success and achievement that you would not have attained had it not been for God's grace and your hard work. And remember that you can't mix lethargy and complacency with growth and happiness, as opposites don't attract!

### What should I do?
Courage is like a muscle: the more you use it, the stronger it gets
- ‣ Think of something you want to change or improve, or a bad habit you want to get rid of. Just one thing
- ‣ Gradually get out of the comfort zone (baby steps): what can I do, or stop doing, every day, to change

for the better? What can I learn, how can I perfect my skills, what are some easy things I can do? Precipitation rarely yields good results, so be sure to adapt to change and leave your comfort zone gradually. Don't sign up for twenty language courses, don't change an unhealthy diet overnight and don't do vigorous workouts every day
➤ Encourage yourself: every day you commit to a resolution you made, tell yourself that you are building your courage muscles and working to raise your self-confidence

**What should I read?**
*Change One Thing!*, by Sue Hadfield.

# Goals bring Happiness

I liked what Abdulla Al Muhairi wrote:
Imagine that you're sitting in a football field, waiting for a game between two of your country's finest teams. The game starts, the teams start attacking and scoring goals, the crowd is excited and starts singing and chanting, everyone singing to their own tune – meaning every side is cheering for their team! Suddenly, amid the chaos, two groups of young men head for the goalposts, grab them and leave the field with them! Now that the stadium doesn't have any more goalposts, do you think the players will keep playing? How will they play? Where will they score? Of course, they will stop playing. But imagine if the referee insists on continuing the game, how will the players spend the ninety minutes of game time? With no more goals and arbitrary playing, fans won't stay at the stadium to watch a goalless game.

Life is just like a game: you're the player, your life goals are the goalpost, the ethics, customs and laws you must respect are the boundaries of the football field, the coach is every person who guides and tries to benefit you, the obstacles you face in life are the opponent team, the players on your team are your friends and those who walk the path of life alongside you, and the referee is each individual who points you to your mistakes. When you score a goal, it means you achieved a life goal. Before the game starts, plan to reach the target and score the highest percentage of goals. You must also train and practise so that you use your training during the match.

What sets successful and happy people apart from others?

The answer is: goals. A happy person sets goals, works towards achieving them, and looks forward to them, even if they're not guaranteed.

***Ask yourself:***
***Do you have life goals, or are you letting yourself drift with the tide of life?***

Happy people are purposeful, not allowing themselves to be scattered or random. They know what they're doing and why. Indeed, one of the most important benefits of having goals is that they help us live in the present and liberate us from the past. Happiness is in the journey! Ask yourself: do you have life goals or are you letting yourself drift with the tide of life? A person with no clear goals might feel happiness but only temporarily; because over time, not having a purpose around which your thoughts, your work and your life centre will make you feel meaningless and reinforce negativity in your life. Having a purposeful life with achievements, goals and work increases your happiness. Even if such a life is exhausting, hard work might exhaust you, but not working is even more taxing and bothersome, because your life would lack meaning! This is what revealed to one scientist the secret behind many people having anxiety and depression during long vacations and after retirement. The reason is lack of purpose.

No purpose no positive feelings, and no positive feelings no happiness, because you experience positive feelings when you live in the present, and thus your conscious or subconscious mind notices that you are moving towards your goals.

***Goals don't just motivate you to move forward, they also give your life meaning and give you positive feelings.***

If you don't have any goals, how will you have positive feelings! Positive feelings occur when you move towards your goals, and satisfaction comes when you achieve them. Goals drive you forward, and as it has been said, "You can't push someone up a ladder unless they want to climb it themselves." The same thing applies to you: you won't move forward in life unless there's a motivator to push you forward, and goals are a person's biggest motivation. Goals don't just motivate you to move forward, they also give your life meaning and give you positive feelings.

**How do I discover my goals?**
There are many ways to discover your life goals, such as:
- Begin with the end in mind: Picture yourself on your deathbed – God forbid – looking back on your life. What do you wish you had done in your family life, your professional life, academically, socially, and spiritually? What would give you satisfaction? What would you wish to tell your spouse and children about your greatest achievements?
- Your goals will start to appear; write them down, review them, and rank them in order of importance.
- What to do in my free time? Define your interests; think of activities you enjoy doing in your free time,

and during which time flies. Write them down on a piece of paper, and don't ignore any of them even you think it's insignificant. Many people don't know that their hobbies can become a huge success and a satisfying goal, if they give them enough attention and excel at them

➤ Avoid distractions and ask yourself: what are the goals I want to accomplish? Who do I want to be; what do I want to do, or own, or achieve in my life, my relationships, my faith and my studies? Whatever your goals may be, know them, remember them, keep your eyes on them and make sure they're a part of your life and your actions

# The Law of Exponential Growth

Even more important than knowing your goals is moving towards them. So, take a daily step – however small – that brings you closer to your goals. If you want to be a distinguished reader, read even as little as five pages a day. If you want to lose weight, walk at least twenty minutes a day. If you want to become a professional programmer, write at least ten code lines daily. And if you want to be a righteous son or a good friend, take daily action, and take the first step, believing in it. You don't have to see all the stairs, just go up to the first step.

Reading one page eventually leads to reading a whole book, and walking twenty minutes eventually results in an athletic, fit body, since small, continuous improvement yields amazing results. Did you know that if you improve your speaking skills every day by one per cent, you will become an outstanding speaker within two months?

> ***You don't have to see all the stairs,***
> ***just go up to the first step.***

For instance, in your everyday life, you shouldn't read a book daily, nor weekly! Forget these big numbers, just focus on the simple things that work miracles over time. If you dedicate 15 minutes to reading every day, you will read 18 books a year. Then you will join the list of 20% of people with the highest reading average in the world.

In your spiritual life, if, before one of your daily prayers, you dedicate ten minutes to reading the Quran, you will read it six times a year.

In your social life, simple things can improve your relationships and make you popular. A simple smile every day, a word of encouragement, a nice WhatsApp message, congratulations on a special occasion: these little, consistent actions can make a huge difference in your relationships over time.

***The secret to achieving goals lies in continuous, simple actions, and this applies to all aspects of your life.***

As for your relationship with yourself, take five minutes before bedtime to remember your blessings and thank God for them. This will change your way of thinking, increase your optimism, improve your health and rid you of negative thoughts. The secret to achieving goals lies in continuous, simple actions; this applies to all aspects of your life. Don't underestimate daily improvement, however small, because its results are astounding. As the Prophets says, "the most regular and constant deeds even if they were little". Just by taking the first step, you would have done the hardest part and broken the psychological barrier. Remember that goals get accomplished only when we work on them. With each step you take in their direction, they grow closer, and your mission becomes easier; for a journey of a thousand miles begins with a single step.

Hence, it's important to set aside a place for your goals in your daily schedule because they will multiply your happiness. Start small, as trying to accomplish huge things

in the beginning is discouraging. Apply the principle of horse training: start with the easiest hurdles. Success doesn't come overnight, by a stroke of luck. Rather, it's gradual. Remember that your goal only brings you happiness if you take two steps:
- ➤ Know it
- ➤ Move towards it and incorporate it to your daily life

# Growth Mindset and Fixed Mindset

I'm such a big fan of table tennis that I became a pro at it. One day, at the gym, I met a nice man and we started playing daily matches. I won at first, but then I noticed something odd: he was always trying out new moves while I stuck to the ones I knew, which had guaranteed my victory so far. I was afraid to try new moves that I hadn't mastered and risk losing game points. But my friend had a principle, which he shared with me: "I focus on learning and having fun rather than winning!" Soon enough, his method started paying off; he kept getting better, while I remained on the same level, and that made him surpass me despite my professionalism.

***Those who have a fixed mindset believe that their skills and intelligence are stable and unchangeable, and that their shortcomings are impossible to get rid of.***

This is the difference between two mentalities: the growth mindset and the fixed mindset. It has nothing to do with intelligence but with the way we think. Indeed, we all have a lifelong ability to learn, improve, evolve and be happy. Those who have a growth mindset excel, and we all know people who we think are less intelligent but more daring and bigger risk takers than us. They handle failure well, even learning from it and improving until they eventually achieve what they want.

This talk about different mindsets isn't theoretical, as it affects your life, your behaviour, your decisions, your perception and the way you deal with others.

- ‣ Those who have a fixed mindset believe that their skills and intelligence are stable and unchangeable, and that their shortcomings are impossible to get rid of
- ‣ Those with a growth mindset believe that their talent, their potential and their life can improve through action, learning, discovery and reflection
- ‣ Those with a growth mindset know that people have different abilities and talents, but that everyone can improve and change for the better with time
- ‣ Those with a fixed mindset run away from situations, relationships and challenges, while those with a growth mindset interact with them and benefit from them

***Someone with a growth mindset focuses on learning. So even if he makes a mistake, he considers it a step that he can benefit from.***

The problem with the fixed mindset is that it makes the owner scared of new situations and challenges because they're afraid that their flaws will be exposed. Hence, he stays away from any novelty, unknown situation, social event and challenging job. His only life goal, which disturbs him and drains his energy and effort, is to prove himself and his intelligence! Someone with a fixed mindset doesn't venture into new challenges or difficult situations. He's evasive, because he's ashamed and afraid of being embarrassed or looking stupid, and he doesn't want others to think of him that way.

## GROWTH MINDSET AND FIXED MINDSET

For example, sometimes a student wants to ask his teacher a question in class; yet he doesn't. Why? Because he's worried that his teacher or his classmates will think: "How stupid is he!"

Conversely, someone with a growth mindset focuses on learning. So even if he makes a mistake, he considers it a step that he can benefit from. You don't see him worry about proving his intelligence or proving himself to others, because he thinks intelligence can be improved. Thus, he focuses on learning and getting better.

The growth mindset is instinctual. Indeed, when a child starts trying to walk and falls repeatedly, he doesn't stop learning, or feel ashamed of other people, he just keeps trying. Similarly, when he's learning to talk, even with eloquent people around, he isn't ashamed or afraid of his level.

These are self-imposed obstacles that appeared over time. We ourselves put these imaginary obstacles made of fear, shame and hesitation.

One researcher asked his students to study the life of the famous and successful before they made it. The students were surprised that all these people went through hard times, had a modest life at first, and were hard-working and diligent.

So, the idea that "successful people are born gifted or social" is worthless. Because the world is full of homeless talented people.

**What is your mindset?**
We all have a mix of both mindsets. You might have a fixed mindset in one area of your life and a growth mindset in another. That's why we need to be aware of our thought process during important times in our life:

- What happens when you face an obstacle? Do you cower in fear, or do you remain calm, analyse, think, advance or retreat, and decide what you can learn?
- What happens if you make a mistake? Do you criticize, blame and scold yourself, or do you consider it a teachable experience and a lesson?
- What happens if someone criticizes you? Do you get angry and defend yourself, or do you think it's his opinion and that you can benefit from it, or ignore it?
- What happens if you realize that someone is better than you? Do you feel bothered and jealous and belittle yourself, or do you get excited and think of ways to learn from him?

So, watch yourself in these moments, and pay attention to your feelings and decisions in these situations. They are what elevate you to a growth mindset.

# Don't Give Up

- Abdul Aziz bin Laboun failed middle school, then changed the course of his life to become one of the most prominent geologists in the world
- Sami Al-Rasheed failed seven times before he succeeded and became a partner in Smaat, one of the largest advertising companies today
- Engineer Ali Al-Qahtani was robbed of his first project, he failed and his losses multiplied. But this theft motivated him to devote himself to commerce and resign from his job
- J. K. Rowling, author of the worldwide phenomenon Harry Potter, was rejected by 12 different publishers and had to wait patiently for a whole year before a publishing house finally accepted her manuscript
- Famous tradesman Al Bassami went through a difficult childhood. He left his parents behind at an early age for the city of Riyadh, where he struggled, working as an employee in the daytime and a taxi driver at night, until he became the owner of the largest fleet of car transport in the Middle East

*Happy and successful people have a strong sense of purpose, which is why the word "surrender" isn't in their vocabulary.*

What do many successful and happy people in various

fields – commerce, science, creativity, etc. – have in common? It's the desire for achievement, persistence and not giving up. They may fail, go through hard circumstances, be ridiculed and criticized, or feel down. But they never give up on their goals, no matter the pitfalls, difficulties and hardships they're exposed to. Happy and successful people have a strong sense of purpose and long to achieve a meaningful life, which is why the word "surrender" isn't in their vocabulary.

This success can mean getting rid of a bad habit, undertaking a business venture, building a strong and stable family, being a righteous son, communicating with relatives or contributing to a project. Whatever your life goals and ambitions may be, remember that successful people don't give up easily.

***Whatever your goal is and whatever success means to you, you will only achieve what you want through persistence.***

Happy people are ambitious and never lose sight of the goals they want to achieve. This means that their perspective doesn't allow them to sink into negative thinking when faced with tough circumstances. Indeed, their motto is: "When the going gets tough, we will surely find a way out of the predicament we're in." Their guide on this path is none other than the Prophet (may peace be upon him): "By God, if they were to place the sun in my right hand and the moon in my left hand in order for me to abandon this matter, I would never do so until God makes it manifest or I die defending it."

## *Persistence = strong desire + continuous work + positive thoughts*

Whatever your goal is and whatever success means to you, you will only achieve what you want through persistence. The bigger your goals and dreams, the more obstacles you will face. As we have seen repeatedly, obstacles are beneficial and can turn into blessings. They're a way to improve and change for the better and a path towards happiness. The road to heaven is paved with hardships. So, be persistent and face any obstacle you encounter in order to overcome it and learn from it, always keeping your eye on your goals. This world belongs to the happy, the dreamers and the ambitious.

**WHAT SHOULD I DO?**

Write down your life goals.

- Take a moment to yourself and think about what you want to accomplish in life. Write down all the goals and thoughts that come to mind. Write a long-term goal and a mid-term one in each of these areas: personal, family, social, academic, professional, faith
- Write down every goal, provided that it is specific, within a reasonable period of time, achievable and measurable. For instance, instead of writing, "I will lose weight," write "In the next month I will lose six pounds."
- Write down how you will achieve this goal; what steps will you take to accomplish it?

| Goal | Area | Type | Steps |
|---|---|---|---|
| Teach a model lesson on the subject of diacritical marks | Professional | Mid-term | Search for previous lessons on the Internet. Request a form to submit the lesson from the supervisor. Buy a book. |
| Obtain the award for "Outstanding Teacher" | Professional | Long-term | Give 3 model lessons. Get my students to win the Riyadh schools competition. |
| Lose six pounds | Health | Mid-term | Walk for half an hour, three times a week. Skip breakfast five days a week. Have a healthy lunch. |
| Increase social interaction | Social | Long-term | Visit aunts and uncles monthly. Write a weekly message (of congratulations, or to check in) to relatives. |

## WHAT SHOULD I READ?

*The Success Factor*, by John Leach.
*Play a Bigger Game!*, by Rowdy McLean.